Praise for *Butterfly Stitches*

I0623731

Michele has written a book which is honest and authentic. Use this book as a guide to getting real with the kind of issues you are facing which have slowed you down or tripped you up.

—*Bob Goff, Author* Love Does

Michele Vrabel has faced heartache, trauma, and generational pain. She has also triumphed. With patience, prayer, surrender, and grit, Michele is partnering with Jesus to craft beauty from ashes. I'm grateful to know her and for this remarkable book.

—*Kimberly Stuart, author of* Star For Jesus (And Other Jobs I Quit): Rediscovering the Grace That Sets Us Free

Michele Vrabel has crafted a poignant memoir of her life, showing us her wounds, stitches, and healing. We cannot comprehend true healing without first seeing the depth of a wound. In this book, you will go back to the beginning, where the first of many betrayals cuts its way deeply into the heart of an innocent little girl. Michele meets Jesus, that very One who is able. His love is transformative, healing years of torment with His perfect presence. Michele lets the reader experience the profound transformation of this ideal, unconditional love! In this book Michele and the reader find our way through together. Sometimes, the only way is through. Through the pain, with healing, stitches and scars; we wear our stories like tattoos. They are wounds that have become a beautiful testament to the goodness of God. We are meant to share these stories to connect to others.

—*Amanda Schaefer Author, Speaker, Global Podcast Host of "A Cup of Gratitude"*

Michele Vrabel's story shows us God's heart is to leave the ninety-nine and go after the one to seek and save those who are lost. In Butterfly Stitches, Michele gives us a memoir that's a raw, unvarnished telling of her painful childhood, her self-described prodigal choices, and her Savior who continued to woo her to Him. Thank you for sharing your story, Michele, that it might be a testimony to others.

—*Lisa Appelo, author of* Life Can Be Good Again

Butterfly
STITCHES

The Metamorphosis
OF HEALING

a memoir
PART I

michele evette vrabel

ISBN: 979-8-9908647-0-2 (paperback)
ISBN: 979-8-9908647-1-9 (digital)

Cover and book design by Melissa Williams Design

Photography: Lindsey Wheeler

Makeup: Amber Wintrow

Contents

Foreword

by John and Robert Vrabel

(Michele's Brothers)

Dear Reader,

I am John Thomas—John or JT to others—and Michele's younger brother. She mostly calls me John, though occasionally for effect, she uses "Doughnut." Don't ask where that childhood nickname came from; she and Bob readily admit they don't remember its origin—they're old and forgetful. Our parents, Madelyn Kay and Roger Francis, made us and named her Michele Evette. Suffice it to say, there is family and life history that we have shared and witnessed, and others that we have not. There are experiences and points of view that we may not have and may not share with each other...but probably should.

    An admission of my own: I had always thought her middle name was Yvette, with a Y. I had never seen her birth certificate because there hadn't been a need. I picked that Y up from an old

Hollywood movie I watched with our adoptive grandmother, Eva Alberta, during one of many summer stays with her and Grandpa Robert William in our younger years. Michele had these summer stays as well. The movie was black-and-white, about a French cavalier. In the credits, his love interest was Yvette, and I thought how lovely it was. I wondered why she didn't like her middle name. Again, we all have our own experiences, mistakes, and omissions that we may wrestle with until we speak them and unburden ourselves.

In the pages that follow, Michele speaks to a journey marked by pain, resilience, and profound healing. I've witnessed firsthand many of her traits through our years coming of age, such as anger, sorrow, ferocity, and tenacity—qualities that propel her life and story, a spirit forged in the baptism of her life's most challenging moments. From the stark clarity of that split-second impact on the baseball field to the deeper wounds etched across the frontier of her life.

This is her invitation into a narrative that transcends mere recounting. *Butterfly Stitches* is more than a memoir; it is a testament to the transformative power of her faith, introspection, and the unwavering presence of a guiding light through the storms.

Also, in these pages, Michele lays bare the scars that bear witness to both inflicted pain and self-inflicted wounds, offering a meditation on the nature of profound healing. Through her journey, she reveals not only the raw reality of abuse but also the profound truth that healing is a journey of surrender and rediscovery—a journey guided not by self, but by a divine grace that stitches together the torn fabric of her life with a strength born of adversity.

As you embark on this poignant exploration of resilience and redemption, prepare to be moved and inspired. Michele's voice resonates with authenticity and grace, offering a beacon of hope to all who have known suffering and sought solace in the healing touch of the Creator.

May this memoir serve as both a testament and a guiding light for those who walk a similar path—a reminder that within the scars of our past lies the potential for profound transformation.

-JT

* * *

I'm Robert Vrabel. The older brother of my siblings Michele and John.

I am also a player in the early tragedy side of the story Michele has put forth. We were the unfortunate offspring of a paranoid schizophrenic father for whom violence and abuse were a normal parenting tool. Reading it conjures so many memories.

I guess I was "lucky". My abuse was only physical (beatings), verbal, and mental. Lucky.

This is the story from her perspective. Our interpretations being like multiple people seeing an accident does not take away from the fact the accident occurred. Just that our memories of the event are different. She was the little girl in the neighbor's yard across the street when my mother was nearly beat to death. I was the little boy banging at the front screen door crying and screaming as I listened to her taking the beating.

Once we told our father to never see us again, my part of the story changed. With regret, the trials and tribulations Michele experienced after that I was either woefully ignorant or too caught up in my own life to give it much mind time.

School, peers, adolescence, young adulthood, life. We never sat down and had a discussion of what we went through. Instead we went to our respective corners and dealt with it each in our own way. When I went into the service and left home the insulation from events became even greater.

It has only been in the last few years that details began to emerge. Coincidently about the same time she started writing this book. New revelations and confirmation of some things I privately thought but never actually expressed. Difficult memories, personal reflections and conviction.

If there was one silver lining in all this is that it produced in me and my siblings a heightened pursuit of achievement. I don't mean the bad kind. We have all gone on to successful careers. Raised beautiful children, who have given us grandchildren and grand nieces and nephews. And we did it without violence or abuse. The chain has been broken.

Through her faith and Christ laying a plan on her heart Sis has laid her life bare. Through that same faith she has given grace and forgiveness. (I'm still working on that part).

If after reading this and you are also a victim of the same style of abuse, take heart. You are not alone anymore. There is no longer the stigma that this must be hidden. Resources are available.

And then there is Jesus. Try him first.

-BOB VRABEL

Introduction

The pitch was coming fast. The bat got a piece of it. It was a split second and slow motion, and I could see it coming and could not avoid it at the same time. Knocked to the ground off my heels and staring up at a blue sky. I knew this kind of pain. There would be blood and some kind of stitches.

There is a split in the skin directly through my left eyebrow. Thanks to the underlying bone, not deep enough to require anything but a butterfly stitch. It held the area together while the healing began. A line where the original scar took up space remains today.

Healing never returns things "back to normal." Because I was created to value and fight for my life, for my health; emotionally, spiritually, mentally, and physically, the healing puts things back stronger.

Looking back through the stitches, to tell my story, magnified where the healing began each and every time. The wound wreaked havoc. My heart and mind began the examination to see how deep the scar would be. My Jesus showed me how to clean out the wound by helping me see what truly caused it and how to grow in the navigating.

I cannot say that at two years old I understood how the Holy Spirit was working in and through me. But I felt it. I could see that I had been reasoning it out, even then.

I am not telling my story to say that no one experiences a one-time come-to-Jesus healing. I am telling my story for those who do not. For those who have not stopped to write it down and see . . . there was Jesus.

It is hard and feels like it will never work out for good for anyone . . . especially me. Life is hard. More of my wounds and stitches came at my own hands and required the same metamorphosis of healing as those at the hands of others.

Butterfly Stitches is not a self-help story. Self never did me a lick of good. Getting out of my own way and realizing that true healing was going to begin with the One who created me.

Butterfly Stitches is the story of seasons of abuse as told by the wounds of my heart, soul, mind, and body in a teaching memoir. Each having witnessed a life from a different perspective. Some experiences looked similar, some completely different, but all create the total of a life.

Season I

IN THE NAME OF LOVE

Chapter 1

Evildoers

"The face of the LORD is against evildoers, To cut off
the memory of them from the earth."

(Psalm 34:16)

I was beaten as a small child by the earthly father that I thought
was supposed to love me. Astonishingly, I worried more about
my mother as she was beaten before my eyes than I did about
myself.

I remember all of the beatings. Particularly those crafted
especially for me.

I was two years old. I was playing in the neighbor's yard
across the street. I am not sure why I was by myself. Angry
shouts were coming from my house. This did not even give me
pause. After what seemed like an eternity of shouting echoing

in my ears, the front door opened. My father stormed across the yard . . . across the street . . . I started to shake. The beeline was straight for me.

He yanked me up from the ground by one arm. The blows across my face were with an open hand. He lowered me and dragged me for a few steps and then back to my face. This pattern was repeated all the way back to the house and down the hallway to my bedroom. My mother was literally thrown aside as she attempted to intervene. After the final blows to my face were administered, I was flung onto my bed. The lights were turned off and I was left there in the dark.

The first blow had been struck to my tender heart. It was working overtime to understand. Wasn't this Daddy? Weren't he and Mommy supposed to love me? Be nice to me? Clearly, I didn't have the vocabulary at age two to understand evil, sin, and directly who God was. Someone helped me understand, even at a young age, that this was not my fault. I didn't hide or stuff it down. I just knew it wasn't about me.

* * *

During the '60s, there were no women's abuse shelters or homes where someone could go to get away from an abusive spouse. The Catholic church, which we belonged to as a family, would not hear of someone divorcing or leaving their mate for any reason. My grandparents expressed that my mom should work it out. The police and what social services there were told my mother that a man could do what he liked with his wife and family. She had nowhere to go, no money to go anywhere, and three children under the age of five. Divine intervention lent a hand.

I was only five when all hell broke loose. I was standing in the front yard of the neighbor across the street again. The woman who lived there had no children and loved having me come over to play. She probably liked my brothers, too, but since this is my story . . . she liked having me over.

Out of nowhere, police cars and an ambulance came roaring up to our house. Time froze for what seemed like an eternity . . . then there was finally movement.

Two adults in uniforms rolled a gurney out to the ambulance with a body on it. I could not see who it was and could not process it even after it all ended. My father was then led out with police officers on both sides and his arms behind his back. I would be told later what transpired.

It took nearly being killed to make my mother accept the possibility that being homeless and on the street was a better option than staying in this house. The details of how we survived during and after the fallout was for the adults to understand. All I knew was once the dust settled, and she was out of the hospital, we were with my mother and not my father. At least for the moment.

Until that day . . . no one came for us. There was no counseling. There was no jail time. There was no justice or fairness. We did not even talk about it. No one asked if we were okay or needed help. I am not sure if those around us truly knew what was happening at the Vrabel house. But they could not have thought it was a party.

I was not to blame. My mother was not to blame. God was not to blame. In fact, if you spin your wheels trying to lay blame for the abuse you have suffered . . . you will spend your life carrying it, reliving it, and letting your abusers get away with it over and over. My father's choice to make this evil generational is one hundred percent on him.

How my mind and heart were shown healing and the choices I would make going forward were one hundred percent on me. This was not going to be how my life would look. This was not how I was going to behave.

* * *

Soon, my brothers and I would be sitting in a courtroom hearing all the gory details of our parents' marriage and how the state of Michigan was going to make us go on visitation with the father that beat the hell out of us regularly and almost killed our mother. Especially at five years old, this was disturbing.

Our father was granted visitation rights by the state. He was technically supposed to pay child support in return. It never materialized. Not one dime. While we went on visits, we were rarely in a genuine relationship with our father. The beatings continued on a lesser scale, and some sexual overtures reared their ugly heads as I matured.

An incident with my father when I was in elementary school turned on competitiveness academically that walked right up to the line of unhealthy. It was his weekend, and on the way to his house when he stopped for dinner at a restaurant with me and my brothers. I was excited about and had just received my report card. It contained all "As" as was my custom, and I blurted it out. My father told me that I was nothing special and I would never amount to anything without him. I was told to shut up and eat. My brothers, Bob and John, looked terrified, as they knew the signs. Signs both of my father's anger and my desire for approval. I was not generally outspoken at this time, since it had gotten me beaten in the recent past.

I suddenly decided to let the scenario in my head come tumbling out. I had overheard my paternal grandfather state that my father's grades in school were barely a "C" average.

The world felt like everything suddenly went into slow motion. My father did not have a poker face, a trait I inherited, and was telegraphing his anger. I do not comprehend why I did not move. My mouth got me promptly backhanded by my father, causing me to do an actual roll over backwards over my chair. I was in a green dress with flowers that my mother had made for me, which was now around my shoulders.

We were at fine dining establishment, and this caused all the diners to stop and gasp. The silence was deafening, and the slow motion returned. The previous sounds of silverware clinking on plates were muted. My ears were ringing, and I only saw mouths moving. My father never paused his eating. When the staff tried to get me up, he yelled at them to leave me be. Blood was running from my mouth and nose, and I was made to sit down and finish my dinner. A Salisbury steak and baked potato, which were incredibly hard to eat with a split lip.

More wounds. More blood. Only deep enough to require a butterfly stitch. Definitely deep enough to leave a scar.

* * *

Generally when we went to our father's house, the first night, Friday, would be spent going out to eat somewhere that typically had a teaching moment attached to it by our father. Saturday would involve rising later and hanging out around the house or on occasion going to a cultural event.

Saturday evening was exclusively for dropping us off at the home of our father's friends while our father and his new wife and the parents of this family went out somewhere. The adults usually came back loud and staggering, and that made for an exciting drive back to the house. This went on for years until after one particularly perilous visit, I decided for myself to say enough is enough.

They came back from wherever "out" was and were in no condition to remain upright, let alone drive. No one in my immediate family drank, so while I knew they looked impaired, I was not prepared for what that would look like behind the wheel of a car. In large cities in Michigan, and I suppose other cities as well, when you are driving on the freeway, the concrete embankments were sloped. We would usually be headed home in the wee hours so there was not much traffic, praise the Lord. My father was not just swerving on the road this time, he was going several yards up the embankment with each swing as well. My older brother was the only one with me on this occasion, and we were terrified. I literally could not take any more of this, and I had no idea how to make it stop. Our father was not bonding with us, and it felt unsafe.

The ride back to my home was tense. You could have cut the silence with a knife. We pulled to a stop in front of our trailer for our father to drop us off. I decided to tell him that I did not wish to do this anymore. I did not feel loved or wanted during these visits. It was an odd ritual, and I was not even sure why he wanted to keep it up.

My mother and younger brother had come out on the porch because we were sitting there for a while as I explained my feelings. As I finished my thoughts . . . he simply popped the trunk for us to get our luggage and very matter-of-factly said, "Okay."

My ears were ringing like when you are going to faint. He didn't ask why. He didn't try to talk me out of it. He didn't say he would miss me or that he loved me. They say the opposite of love isn't hate, it is apathy.

His wife, wearing a cast on her arm and a bandage over a broken nose from her own treatment at the hands of our father, started screaming at me and indicating that I was listening to my horrible mother. As a child I had always been respectful of my elders and never talked back. I kind of lost my mind at this point. I yelled at her to shut up. I told her to "look at him," meaning my father. He showed no emotion at all. I told her I had my own mind and that these visits were not even about a relationship with him at all. My brother and I then got out of the car. I found out later that my older brother had been silently cheering me on. We got our luggage, closed the trunk, he pulled away, and we never saw him again.

* * *

In spite of all that I had been through, this was a wound that did not heal quickly. My relationship with Jesus was developing, and that was what I needed to fill the gaps that were left by the rejection of my earthly father. Jesus gave me the emotional "stitches" to pull the pieces of my heart back together. To seek him where a father's counsel was needed.

Well-meaning individuals decided they had a right to condemn me for never seeing my father again. For not wanting the abuse to continue. Assuming unforgiveness. I have been informed that I am not Christian for walking away. My God gives us the ability to get a certificate of "divorce" when infidelity and abuse are present. He gave me the presence of mind, as a teenager, to protect myself.

A wound cannot heal in the midst of being torn. While I was not allowed to talk about what was happening, and there was absolutely no one checking on me, I know my King gave me the boldness to remove myself and begin to heal. I forgave my father without ever receiving an apology. I forgave because I was forgiven.

I can give the churchy answer about evil and terrible things happening being a byproduct of free will. I can talk about the fall and the impact this had on God's decision to allow us free will. And while this all is true, the fact of the matter is . . . we all make choices. We all decide to either choose evil or good. My father made his choices. Unfortunately, we all suffered the consequences. None of us sins in a vacuum. If you have been a victim of abuse, reconciling someone else's evil choices will be your ultimate test about grace, forgiveness, and peace. Anything other than this will only allow the abuse to travel with you like luggage.

My King has kept every promise. He promised not to intercede on the free will He has given us all. He promised not to ever leave or forsake us either. He never left me. He was giving me everything I needed to survive and work out better choices for myself.

♡ 10

Chapter 2

Unaware

Bonus Dad—one who made the choice to love
another's child as their own.

–Unknown

She was small but not fragile. My mother's recovery from the near-fatal beating my father gave her kept her at the hospital for several months for some physical therapy. She met a kind man, Richard, who had been injured in a construction site accident. My mother never disclosed details about how they met, and I never asked. Once she came home and we were together again, he just started coming around.

They dated for a while as he slowly became a part of our new family. My mother moved the four of us into an apartment where he would visit and have dinner with us. He understood what environment we had come from and did not try to force a relationship with any of us. He was a gentle giant and showed us kindness as a man, kindness that to this point we had only seen from our grandfather.

Richard had two daughters of his own who were close in age to me and my brothers, and he was very tender-hearted toward me. He saw my hesitance to speak to anyone, particularly adult males. He would ask me if I wanted to go for a ride to the car wash, and along the way he would talk to me without expecting a response. He would then take me to get an ice cream cone and considered my little smile a victory. He was making great inroads in establishing a relationship with us kids.

His brother came to town to pay him a visit, and after coming to our apartment for dinner a couple of times, my mom and her boyfriend Richard decided he would make a good after-school babysitter for us, since he didn't have a job.

He was a grown man who was extremely overweight that would stare at me with a creepy smile. He planned out how to keep my brothers occupied in the living room and isolate me in the bedroom. My brothers would be parked in front of the television with a sack full of candy. He knew that I had come from an abusive situation and threatened to beat me if I resisted and offered candy if I complied. He was twenty-three years old, and I was five.

His size made this all the worse for me regarding pain. My little mind could not process why this was happening or what it was. No one else had ever done this to me. Another adult male, not necessarily supposed to love me, but put in authority over me as a "babysitter" chose to abuse.

He sexually molested me for over a year. He was molesting

one of his other brother's two daughters at this time as well. It took the older of the two speaking up to make it stop.

This man was not brought to justice. The man my mother was dating and his entire family had a meeting. The parents of the pervert begged for mercy for this sick, evil man. He molested me and two of his nieces, and they begged for leniency for him.

The final decision to make the adults involved feel better allowed for the near-fatal beating of the abusive brother. No thought was given to any of the young girls' trauma. I do not recall anyone ever discussing it again, especially me. You did not talk about any of this at that time in our society. I had not had one bit of therapy or counseling from any avenue for anything I had gone through in my childhood. Therapy was considered unheard of and unnecessary.

This wound remained open and unattended as I dealt with the processing of the emotions my tender heart was walking through. I was struggling to find any grown-ups who were behaving in a way that not only considered me but was not doing me harm. It did create in me the ability to truly see the galactic difference between good and evil, love and apathy, and how to start protecting myself.

* * *

We left the scene of the crime. My mother found a house in Lansing for all of us and our soon-to-be stepfather. Richard was a kind man; however, my heart was still scrambling to understand all of the recent events. I am not sure of his relationship with my brothers, but he seemed to take special care of how he and I would move forward.

Shortly after our move, they made the decision to marry. We were all in our "church" clothes and went to a place where

13 ♡

there was another judge. My grandparents were there to take us kids back to the house while my mother and her new husband had their honeymoon at a local hotel.

It was Super Bowl weekend, and my mom and stepfather decided to have us kids come to the hotel where there was a good size television to watch the game. I did not fear my stepfather, but heading into a hotel brought trepidation to mind from my last visit to one which included my father.

My stepfather was not a perfect man, and well, who is? He took really good care of us and particularly of our mom. He had two daughters from a previous marriage, and when they did get to visit, it was really fun having other females in the house. When they would leave, I would get the doting of my stepfather and his loving attempts to bring me out of my safe little shell. I believe the guilt of what his brother had done to me weighed on him throughout our relationship.

The couple of years we spent in Lansing seemed like normal family stuff for the most part. Going to school and playing extracurricular sports. Playing with our friends in the streets until the streetlights came on and we had to head home. Drive-in movies in the summer and bowling teams in the winter were the "Michigander" things to do, and we had no idea we were poor or missing anything. In fact, I am not sure that we were. We had anything that was necessary, and we were happy and healthy. For me and what would become a lifetime of some type of abuse, this felt like a less-shaky foundation.

* * *

My time in elementary school was coming to a close, and we were to sit down for a family discussion. We were going to move again. My grandfather had a lake property, near Decatur, Michigan, where he had built a home for himself and my grandmother to retire. It was a couple acres, and there was a single-wide trailer across the dirt road from their house which would be our new home. Because of the location, I am assuming that was why we chose where we did.

Prior to our home in Lansing, we had moved several times, and the broken little girl in me reverted to her introverted little shell every time. I had loosened up and was a little more foot-loose for a while; however, our move to Decatur was for my junior high years in school, and that caused me to revert to protective territory again.

The property we lived on was very rural, so we needed the school bus to get us to school, which, because we couldn't drive, would be our only opportunity to hang out with other kids. Because we were new and hadn't established many friend-ships yet, the bulk of our time for the first year involved my brothers and me getting into mischief on our own.

Because we were usually on the move after a short time, my trust was low and my walls were high. Due to a shortage of transportation and any kids nearby, I did not establish any new friendships during my middle school years.

Since our new home was even farther away for our father, the visits with him were spaced further apart. They did not, however, end, and with each passing occasion the wounds felt a little more salt.

Chapter 3

Born Once

"The two most important days in your life are the day
you are born and the day you find out why."

–*Mark Twain*

Our weekly sacraments were communion and suffering.

I was born to Catholic parents in Fort Wayne, Indiana. My
maternal grandparents were Lutheran but forgave my father
for my mother's conversion, since he was their choice over a
young man they ran off. I am the middle child and only girl
sandwiched between brothers. My older brother was also born
in Indiana. I was around two years old when we moved to
Lansing, Michigan, at which time my younger brother was
born.

My mother was an adopted only child and we only had

distant cousins on her side. My father was the oldest of three, two boys and a girl. My father and his family were devout Catholics. My father was the product of some pretty intense abuse as a child and young adolescent. As a small child, I got to see my paternal grandfather's personal brand of beating up close as he administered it to my beautiful grandmother.

On one occasion at the family cabin north of Detroit, he was particularly vicious. We were all sitting around a picnic-style dining table for breakfast. I cannot remember who was crying, but I believe it was my younger brother. My grandfather was vocal and nasty about his distaste for "whining and crying." My grandmother stood up to console my brother at which point abruptly . . . and shall I say startlingly . . . my grandfather grabbed a shovel handle he kept near him and took a full swing at my grandmother's head, knocking her to the floor with blood spurting. This began a chaotic chorus of crying from all of us kids.

My mother jumped up to help my grandmother, and both my grandfather and father berated her and told her she would receive the same. My mom had been beaten enough that she knew what was coming for her show of compassion and continued to take care of my grandmother in spite of the threat. More beatings ensued. My grandfather shoved my mother off of our grandmother, while my father worked on eliminating the crying. I wish I could say this was unusual.

This was the world I was born into. This was my introduction to the impact of the evil that one commits affecting more than just themselves. It is truly theirs to own, but the fallout tears at the spirit of the humans in their spheres of influence and truly brings to light the potential abuse has to wound.

Much of what I know about my father's backstory came later while having to sit in a courtroom and hear it read. The physical abuse and beating I learned about up close and personal.

My father usually struck us so that no one could see the bruises. Occasionally he lost control, and it didn't matter as long as his hand or fist found its mark. He would require our mom use makeup, if necessary to cover any visible bruising, in order to make it to church, the Catholic church, every Sunday. This was a week-in, week-out scenario in our home.

I was three years old and dancing in the kitchen in a mint green dress and frilly bottoms that my maternal grandmother had made for me. I had completed my chore of setting the table. I was to fully set the table for breakfast for all of us. There was always a bowl with half a grapefruit in it for my mother and father. There were two small dishes with vitamins for my parents as well.

I heard his voice booming as it came down the hall, preceded by my older brother on the run. This particular rampage was instigated by the need to get our shoes. It was winter, and our shoes and boots were inside the kitchen door that led to the basement. My father would get so worked up shouting that he would froth at the mouth as he barked his orders. I would think in my fragile little mind . . . *please just shut up and hit me.*

As my brother and I were attempting to get our shoes on and apparently taking too long, my father tossed us through the door and down the basement stairs. Crumpled at the bottom of the stairs on the concrete floor, my brother and I were forming our own bond and coping mechanisms as we helped each other up. My busted lip and bruises did not compare with the tear to my soul that this was done at the hands of my father. This would not excuse us from attending church . . . nor from putting on the aforementioned shoes.

The church we attended was in downtown Lansing. The stairs at the entrance were steep like they are on buildings in the city. We were dwarfed by the gigantic wooden doors. The priest in his white robes held the door and watched us walk in like ducks in a row every week. Saw the condition we were in. The same priest who would later reject us and close the door. Inside, it smelled of incense that overwhelmed you upon entering. It was quiet except for the sound of our dress shoes walking to our pew.

We sat in the same pew every Sunday. Everyone did. I stood up and turned around. The nice lady who always sat behind us would wave at me like ladies do. That day, while looking at my bruised face and busted lip, she waved with a tear rolling down her face.

* * *

Every now and then, when my father's brother, my uncle Jack, was home on leave from Vietnam, somehow, he found out what was happening in our home. Later, we would find out a neighbor had been the saving grace reporting to my uncle and the police. We would be in the middle of total chaos—kids screaming, mom being beaten—and the front door would burst open and there would stand my uncle Jack. My real-life Captain America. For right or wrong, he would pull his brother off our mom and beat the living shit out of him. I am sorry to say that my little heart cheered inside as I brought my mom warm compresses to stop the bleeding.

Our reprieve did not last long, but in its odd little way, it made me see that all men were not that way. And that what my father was choosing to do were his own choices. He and my uncle came from the same horrors and yet chose completely different paths.

There was nowhere to go at that time if you were a woman with children, no job, and trying to get away from the abuse. Not the Catholic church, no safe houses. No money, nowhere to go. My grandparents wanted her to work it out with our father.

Finally, when the incident that included an ambulance and police cars took place, we got our first taste of freedom. Our saving grace on this occasion was our babysitter, who was a 6'2" Army sergeant who loved us dearly. She came into the house and pulled our dad off our seemingly already-dead mom and brought the cavalry with her. Finally, the police took action and arrested him.

We had attended the Catholic church every Sunday up to this point. Looking like the perfect family all in a row. Having been beaten and threatened to behave before we went in, even though we already knew and were not making a peep.

One of the worst "religious" points of my childhood consisted of the church throwing us out, or actually not letting us in. It was our first Sunday back after my mom got out of the hospital. Her eyes were blackened, and the splint was still on her broken nose. She had filed for divorce while fighting for her life. My dad had beaten my mom almost to death, and while in the hospital she signed the divorce papers. She took us to church, and the same priest in the white robes who watched us attend each week would not let us enter the church.

"Mommy, why would God do this?" Of course, at my young age who I really meant was the priest.

"You explain to her your decision," she told the priest. He went inside without a word and shut the door in our faces. She remained a devout Catholic even without a church home until her death.

I never again attended Catholic services, with the exception of funerals for loved ones. I do not recall thinking that any specific component of the Catholic church or God was at the helm of this rejection. Their representative saw fit to cast out a woman and her children because authorities at the Vatican said this was law.

This did not cause me to question God. Another man claiming to love in God's name was choosing rejection instead. It was a spiritual wound caused by humans claiming to represent Him.

* * *

Shortly after we were refused entrance to the church, my mom introduced us to a man she met while in the hospital. He had been injured on the job at a construction site. They dated for a couple years while he came to our apartment to visit and to start becoming part of our family.

During this time, both my mother and Richard worked full-time jobs, and we were still a little too young to manage ourselves. Richard's half-brother came to town and did not have a job yet. So, the adults decided that he could be our after-school supervision. He was family, so of course no one was concerned about his character.

I was five years old, and he was twenty-three. He knew exactly what he was doing. He was a predator. He knew what we had been through and how to manipulate us to get what he wanted. He bought candy for us all and planted my brothers in the living room watching cartoons.

For me, he had special plans. He threatened to beat me if I spoke up. A threat he knew would hit its small target. He promised to give me candy and not to hurt my brothers for my silence. I had just been set free from watching my mother, myself, and my brothers being "hurt" against my weak protestations. How did we get out before? Will someone come to help me? He was a huge, disgusting, grown-ass man who knew exactly what he was doing, molesting me. In fact, he was doing the same thing to two of his nieces.

Our apartment was small, and my brothers and I shared one bedroom. We had bunkbeds that were small. He never closed the door which led directly to the living room where my brothers were. He knew his threat silenced me. He pinned me to the lower bunk. He did not get undressed. He just undid his zipper and pulled himself out. I remember along with the pain of a grown man entering me, he had a huge belt buckle that dug into my flesh. I do not remember it taking very long . . . just every . . . single . . . day after school.

I remember vividly one time I broke free of him and ran screaming into the living room, despite his threats, since I wanted it to stop. I tried grabbing my brothers and begging them to help me. He told them we were playing and to go back to watching cartoons as he dragged me back to the bedroom, hysterical.

This went on for a year and a half before one of the older nieces finally spoke up. I cannot even imagine how long this would have gone on if not for her.

Everyone went to the grandparents' home in Cadillac. There was a lot of yelling and begging going on between the adults. I sat on the couch, expressionless, where my knees did not even reach the edge of the cushion. Not truly comprehending the sequence of events. A decision was reached that the family considered justice. For whom I am not sure, but it did not seem like it was for me.

Richard and his older brother, the father of the abused nieces, walked on either side of the pervert and headed outside into the snow. They beat him unconscious. Having been freed from a house of violence, this did not reconcile in my mind as justice being administered.

I was not asked. I was not asked how I felt. I was not asked if I was okay. No one even checked me out physically. There was no counselor. They decided the justice. I was not to speak of it.

Once again, with my little spirit reeling, I was given what I needed to survive the journey. I realize that the Holy Spirit I would later come to know by name, was my comforter . . . my counselor . . . even then.

I never believed that my mom or God or anyone but the evil pervert who did this was at fault. It did, however, make me reek of vulnerability, and that would play into many things as I walked my journey. Over and over, men who were supposed to love me and were put in authority over me . . . did not love or value me at all. The arrogance of the gatekeepers that both closed and left open doors that would shatter my world.

* * *

In my middle school years, an opportunity to attend another type of church presented itself. The man my mom was dating had relatives who were members of the Pentecostal church. This was decidedly the most interesting time of church attendance in my life! It was all the fun things that are stereotypes in the movies, but also just a lively, fun group of people who did love the Lord.

I remember the Sunday school teacher, and she had an incredible gospel presentation that left an impression on me. She took care of all of us under her teaching and expressed true love and desire for us to have a relationship with our Lord and Savior, Jesus.

There was a boy in my Sunday school class who had several

birth defects, one of which was blindness. He was very sweet, and we became fast friends. I felt drawn to him, not out of pity but out of compassion. His level of happiness, in spite of his circumstances, was the definition of joy.

Some of the other children decided that merely picking on him was not enough; they would now include me. This unleashed protective instincts that I did not know I possessed. The precious Sunday school teacher intervened and taught us all about Jesus' love for us . . . for everyone. Even though I had been rejected by those who were supposed to love me here on Earth, this resonated with me because she was pouring out Jesus' love on us, not just saying words. For that hour on those occasional Sundays, she was safe for me. She was the love Jesus had for me. It was extremely interesting, and even then I realized what was Bible-based and truthful about what was going on around me.

A lot of my thinking regarding God was developed very young, and it is amazing that none of it contained negativity toward my King. Somehow, in all of what was going on, I knew that those men were bad. That what they were doing was of their own accord.

God created us for relationship. Relationship with Him and those here with us. He does not force us to love Him or them. He promised us we get to choose. Sadly, we all have the nature to choose what we want at any price and with no regard for the fallout on others.

He also promised to never leave us or forsake us. There was Jesus. From the first blow, my little heart and mind were shown the way to understand that this was not about me. The only reason I am who I am today . . . there was Jesus helping my mind and soul grow into better.

Each wound came with healing. Each wound has left a scar of knowing.

Born Again

"Jesus answered him, 'Truly, truly, I say to you,
unless one is born again, he cannot see
the kingdom of God.'"

(John 3:3)

My photographic memory could give Polaroid a run for its money, but I cannot for the life of me remember my last year of junior high school. We had moved to Decatur, Michigan, for what was about our sixth school change. I struggle to recall anything or anyone from that time. I remember the school building and going into the office to get registered. It was the first time I heard my mother say her birthdate and age aloud. She was almost exactly twenty years old when she had me and was only thirty-three at the time. Funny how our minds work regarding memory. We do not get to choose.

When I headed into high school, I initially sort of fell into the wrong crowd, as they say. I smoked and hung out on the street corners, just looking like trouble. The reality is that I really did not do anything too awful. I smoked for like two weeks and hung out with some kids who brought me into their group because I was the new kid with no place to go and no one laying claim to me.

It was there that one of those friends was behaving as a "groomer" for her cousin. I am not sure how old he was, but he seemed to always be available when we were loitering. He would give us rides wherever we needed to go and buy his cousin and the rest of us cigarettes.

She got in my ear talking him up. She would tell me that he thought I was cute and that he wanted to know me better. She told me that he wanted to do special things with me. She then confessed that she had a special relationship with him, too. She told me that he wanted to take us places and take good care of us. I recall feeling something in my gut that was similar to events of my childhood but had not yet developed the courage to speak up for myself.

They got their opening when one day we were let out of school early, and he promised to give us both a ride home. He had a truck with a bench seat, and they conveniently placed me in the middle. He pulled out of the school and headed in the opposite direction of home. When I questioned them, they promised a fun country ride that would loop around.

At this point she opened the glove compartment and got out a special cigarette that would make me feel good. I had no earthly clue what pot was and did not intend to find out. They lit a joint and both partook while still trying to convince me of its benefits. It did not occur to me that he would be impaired driving, or I would have had one more thing to freak out about.

While they were passing the joint between them, she kept pushing up against me and moving me toward him. I was truly terrified on the inside and was panicking as to what to do. He decided to seize the opportunity of my proximity to slide his hand between my legs. I can honestly say that they were not the only ones surprised by my reaction.

It was full blown hysteria. I was screaming, slapping, and punching. No one got out of that truck unscathed. He slammed on the brakes, and the truck came to a screeching halt at an angle across the center line of the highway. I was grabbing for the door latch on her side. We were in the middle of nowhere, but I wanted out. They were both yelling at me to calm down. Yelling has never calmed me down.

Somehow, we all quieted down. They promised to take me home if I told no one and threatened me with bodily harm if I did. They let me sit next to the door. Their threats to harm me were successful. Not another word was said.

That was the end of the wrong crowd for me.

For another time in my short life thus far, there was Jesus. He was showing me how to see those trying to take advantage of my insecurity. I was having literal physical and emotional reactions to my circumstances that were alerting me to potential damage. The emotional wounds that having those close to me offer me up for no good were not deep but created a scar tissue that would make it harder for those inviting good into my life to get through.

* * *

For a couple of months, I let school and sports be the only interaction I had with others until I got my bearings. Shortly after this, I met my bestie, Bethany. She was sweet and kind of naïve . . . a believer . . . and accepted me on sight. She was adorable, and everything about her was feminine. I was raised with brothers, loved sports, and had very little about me that was feminine. She dressed as you would expect a girl to, and I dressed like a tomboy. Not that I did not like being a girl. I did not want to draw attention to the things that caused me pain.

I loved her, and she and her family loved me. They invited me to their church every chance they got. Being in their home showed me how families were supposed to treat each other. They attributed this to their relationship with God and each other.

Bethany and her mom loved me like I was family and prayed fervently for me. Spending the night at Bethany's house and making homemade divinity are some of my fondest childhood memories. Divinity is no easy task, and her mother loved an extra set of strong arms for holding the mixer.

Bethany and her family were an example of a biblical family. They were not perfect, but they showed me how mothers and fathers were to treat one another as an example to the children in the family. They showed me what living a relationship with the savior was truly like. I loved spending time with them, and they seemed to love having me there, too.

My family was living in a trailer on lakefront property where my grandpa Beberstein had built a retirement home for my grandmother. We were going to have a house built on the property as well. While my grandfather would have preferred that we attend a Lutheran church, he willingly took us to church every Sunday, since he was just happy that we were going to church at all. My grandfather was a sweet, quiet man who never cussed. He was German and had one beer with lunch and one with dinner. He adored my grandmother, loved his family and God, and provided as was his duty.

My grandmother was a pill. She had rules that she formulated out of a combination of backwoods sayings and the Bible. She cussed like a sailor and only drank whiskey, diet Pepsi, and tea. I do not recall ever seeing her drink a glass of water except to take her pills.

Every Sunday as we all were heading for the car, she would be standing on the porch in her housecoat. She wore her "blue hair" in curlers, white face powder, and bright red lipstick. She would have a cigarette dangling out of her mouth as she screamed obscenities at us regarding what we were supposed to wear to church and to hurry up. I have to say it is a miracle Jesus found me right where I was.

* * *

While we had attended church during my childhood, it did not feel like a family. Especially with the beatings and the chaos that took place in our home beforehand. Decatur Bible Church was my first church family. They were my first understanding of how the church was supposed to represent Christ. I attended services every time the doors were open and when my grandfather did not mind driving me. My brothers and I attended all the youth functions and made lifelong friendships.

When school was out in the summer, families with larger houses hosted the youth group Bible studies and social gatherings. Also in the summer was a camping and canoeing trip every year. It began at a lake in the upper part of the lower peninsula of Michigan.

We would canoe for the day and then pull over on the riverbank to a campsite that some of the awesome parents and grandparents would set up, break down, and move each day.

Watching adults care this much about their kids' activities was mind-blowing for me. They cared that their children understood the Bible and what a relationship with Christ looked like. My mother loved us kids and wanted us to be morally upright. She attended our school and sporting events when she could. But when it came to our spiritual health, she had become closed-off after her divorce.

When I was thirteen years old, in April of 1976, a revival group came to our church. My brothers and I attended every night. It was very exciting, and I had never seen anything like it other than Billy Graham on television. I had probably drained the life out of our youth pastor with questions over the preceding two years, and yet I still was working out what a relationship with God was going to look like for me.

Bethany and her mom had prayed over me and answered my endless questions. Her dad was a farmer and a very quiet man. He did, however, speak up to interject when a question demanded his input. He was particularly careful with me due to my experiences with men with authority over me. He was a good man and a great husband and father.

My questions were answered, the Holy Spirit worked in my heart, and it was time. Time to decide if Jesus was for real. The layers of betrayal I had experienced had been hard to cut through. Jesus showed up in my Pentecostal Sunday school teacher . . . in my Bethany . . . in her family and in my church family. He had been showing up my entire life. It was time to make our relationship real. We were going steady.

It definitely was emotional, but that is not all that a salvation experience embodies. It is so hard to explain, and I know the world would have you believe that we are "selling" Jesus or that it is all pulling at heartstrings and scaring you straight so you don't go to hell.

But that is not it at all. It is truly understanding that I am a sinner, born with free will and a sin nature, not perfect . . . and that is okay. God loves me enough that he provides the way for me to have the joy of a relationship with Him and be redeemed to spend eternity with Him because of my precious Lord and Savior, Jesus.

Life is real, and it is hard. Choices do not have a clear-cut path most of the time; we can make choices that appeal to our narcissistic little selves, or we can fulfill our purpose: to both glorify God and serve others. I have never felt unfulfilled or negative about the opportunity to serve others. Nor have I ever regretted it.

I was not promised that life would be easy and always happy. I was promised that trusting that the way God asked me to live and serve Him was the way to a more peaceful and fulfilling existence. My life being joyful and happy comes from the outpouring of my obedience to the will of God.

It is not easy to follow all the time, and there are many times that I chose what sounded better to me and found myself crying out to Him for help getting out of a pickle. Consequences come with every choice we make. Good or bad, there are consequences to our choices and decisions in life.

A smart man learns from his own mistakes; a wise one learns from those of others. I have spent a lot of time in my life having to go through something more than once because I was not wise enough to learn by seeing what others had to go through. I always thought of myself as intelligent. Boy, did God have a sense of humor showing me how "intelligent" I was.

The gaping wounds in my little soul were about to begin the real work of continuing to heal. I had met my Jesus from the first wound, going to church where all could see. Having the door closed by men who believed they were keeping us from God for our mother's sin. Truthfully showing me that we no longer needed an earthly intercessor to come straight into the presence of Jesus.

It's Only Logical

"Logic will get you from A to B.
Imagination will take you everywhere."

–*Albert Einstein*

Three pounds of gray matter working overtime to sort out the world. It is all more than my precious little mind can take. It is amazing how our minds and memories work. There are events in my life, even when I was as young as two years old, that I can recall in microscopic detail. There are short spans where I have nothing. What happened? When I think of the horrors I do remember . . . what happened in the nothing?

After the ambulance pulled away. The police car with my father in the back is driving down the road. Where did we go? It appears we were with our father at some point. My mind is a black hole. Not one image . . . not a flash. If everything I can recall was this much fun . . . what on earth happened in the forgetting?

My father is driving us to the hospital to visit our mother. A tall, blonde woman is in the passenger seat facing forward. We are not introduced, and she does not say a word. The three of us kids are huddled in the back seat of our family car, an old station wagon with a strip of paneling running down each side. The only sound is muffled sobbing and sniffling. As we are riding along, he proclaims our mother is dead, as if announcing what the weather will be that day. It was surreal and terrifying. He seemed almost giddy. We make it to the hospital to discover that thankfully she is not dead. She does, however, look as if barely.

The adults are discussing stuff that sounds serious. A nurse ushers us out of the room. It took a total stranger to make the call that we probably should not hear what is being said.

My father raises his voice, and I begin to quake. My little mind has no idea that people here will stop him. No one ever has. All I know is I could be next. Just the sound of his voice made me feel even the smallest tear in the already gaping wound.

Once again, my little mind is working it out. People around us are interceding on our behalf. I must be right. This is not how he is supposed to act. My Comforter is showing me that He is providing a way out.

My mother has filed for divorce. She is serving our father the divorce papers in the presence of witnesses. Because of the condition our father put her in, the court has awarded her custody and taken us from our father. Apparently, nearly being beaten to death was all it took.

Our maternal grandparents were there for the handoff. I

cannot comprehend how we were placed with our father in the first place. I realize our mother was hospitalized. But, for heaven's sake, our father had been arrested for putting her there. Where was the logic in giving us to him? The police let him go? And everyone involved thought getting to go back home with him was safe for us?

Shortly after getting back home from the hospital, my mother had her court date for the divorce. My older brother and I, at six and five, were deemed able to speak about things and were in the court room for the proceedings. Our younger brother was to go into the judge's chambers.

I was too young to know what some of the terms meant, but they were the sordid details of my father's extracurriculars, and siblings were mentioned. At that moment all I could think to myself was, *Are they getting hurt, too?*

The time came for my mother's side of the story. We would have to speak, too. Apparently, even the court thought we were on our mother's side.

The courtroom smelled old. It was extremely intimidating. Everyone in charge was a man, except for the lady typing and some woman called the "friend of the court." She was supposed to be on us kids' side. All of these men scared the dickens out of me. My mind was chaotic with all of this information and the fact that I would be at the receiving end of their questions soon. Everyone in uniform prior to now had come to our home and done nothing to change our circumstances.

They did not scare me like I thought they would hurt me. It was worse than that. They scared me because I believed they would not help if we were getting hurt again. A public place was not a deterrent for my father.

They literally put books on the chair before hiking me up on the witness stand. I was trembling and did not want to look up and make eye contact with my father. Or for that matter, anyone. They asked me, "Do you know what is going on here?" I meekly nodded even though a part of me thought that was just what I was supposed to do. They asked me, "Do you know what a lie is?" Again, nodding. They made me lay my hand on a Bible and promise not to lie. Funny how at that exact moment everyone else in the courtroom started to.

The judge spoke softly and kindly, but that did nothing to assuage my fears. It was not his fault. He did not know how I had come to be wired. Now the man who had been sitting with my father had his turn. He was harsh. He was shouting his questions. I do not know if he knew he was freaking me out, but it came across like he had an inside track on my father's methods. Tears were streaming down my chubby little cheeks as I tried to answer his questions. They started becoming statements that he was trying to shout me into agreeing with. Why wasn't the man at my mother's table helping me? The judge? The "friend of the court"? See, no one was coming to help.

Finally, the judge intervened. Enough was finally enough. The man in the uniform got me down from my perch on the stand. I ran back to my mother who pulled me onto her lap. She had tissues. She had kids; she always had tissues. They ordered me back to the seat where my brother was waiting for his turn. He was stronger and handled the questions to the best of his ability.

Now the arguing started over visitation and money our father was supposed to pay for us. My father was loud about taking us for more time so he could pay less. My mother was terrified of the possibility of us spending more time with him where the opportunity for hurting us would be more likely. The "friend of the court" commented to my mother, "You should be happy to get rid of your kids every other weekend for a break."

The snap was almost audible. My mother was a tiny woman, 5'4" and 100 pounds soaking wet. I had never seen her full-on angry up to that point. Even with everything our father had put us through. The moment the last word left the mouth of the "friend of the court," all hell broke loose. I had never seen my mother move that fast and yell that loud. She streamed across the courtroom and looked as if she was going to take her out. The men in uniforms came rushing over; the judge was banging his hammer; total chaos.

My brother and I were both freaked out and amazed that our mother had it in her. At this point, they decided that the children should be put in a separate room, which was directly connected to the courtroom by a door.

Decisions were made and the schedule was set. We were to go on visitation with our father every other weekend and longer in the summer. The hammer slammed down. The decision was final. None of our thoughts. None of our words. Nothing made a difference. The man that beat our mother nearly to death was going to get his right to have us every other weekend. Period.

I was too small to truly understand what had just happened. What a divorce was. That our family had just been torn asunder. I was not processing this as a family unit that would not exist anymore. I did not have a lot of loving family memories to make this moment sad for me. The wounds of that part of my heart would very soon be infected with the reality of why we were now living only with our mother.

* * *

My mind had been given the ability to compartmentalize my reality. When the Friday of a visitation weekend came, I adopted silence and would not talk to adults, mostly males, and especially my father in the beginning. I had gone through beatings and verbal berating at the hands of my biological father. This was incredibly hard to reconcile, and the fact that I had to go on visitation after my mother finally accomplished the divorce made this process even harder. My father was also verbally abusive and made us feel worthless and exceptionally so if we were going to go through life without him.

Our father lived in Dearborn, Michigan, and had to travel to get us in Lansing. On several occasions our visitation consisted of us staying at a hotel in Lansing. It is odd what I remember clearly and what has gaps. I remember the woman he married being there almost from the beginning. The woman from the car ride to the hospital.

On one of our hotel visits, my father was quizzing us about various things for school. The television was on and all of us kids were piled on one bed. My father's "lady friend" was sitting at the table. Our father was on the other bed. My younger brother was barely in kindergarten at the time. I do not remember the exact question that was asked of him. I remember vividly every moment after.

It was a combination of my brother not knowing the answer and taking too long to respond. It happened in a split second and yet in extremely slow motion. Our father, with a full fist, punched him straight in the mouth. It was not unusual for our father to beat, whip, or spank us for any reason, at any time. But this startled all of us. His lady friend screamed. Blood was pouring out of my brother's nose. My older brother and I grabbed our brother and formed a barrier.

Hotel guests called the front desk and the police. Our mother was called to get us. I cannot say what actually happened to our father. I do not remember another hotel visitation after that. We did go on visitation for several more years. Always at his home now. Where no one else could hear. The atrocities got worse. Most were in private and are not mine to share.

Our visitation weekends with our father were bizarre, to say the least. I did not feel particularly loved. He never had conversations with us about our lives and what we had going on. He never said, "I love you." He never said, "I am sorry."

On occasion, he took us to culturally relevant events to "teach us" things. There was an international festival at Cobo Hall every year, and we would go if it was his weekend. We would try different foods each year. On one occasion, we were at a Greek restaurant, and he was forcing us to try things we had never eaten. My younger brother insisted on ordering a cheeseburger and chocolate milk, as usual. This brought a new rampage. Our father, yelling, frothing at the mouth. All to teach us about other cultures.

The following year, we were at the Chinese portion of the festival and being told we would eat what was put in front of us once again. I was being forced to eat a shrimp dish. This would be the occasion when we found out I was allergic to shellfish. I did not like the taste or texture to begin with, and my father lost his patience. He literally shoved one in my mouth and shouted at me to eat it. The choking and hives that followed did not dissuade him from his mission.

My mind could not wrap itself around what was happening to us. Why on earth would we be forced to be with this man who found us so intolerable? How was this enjoyable for him either?

I was able to distinguish between the reality of my living situations with each of my parents. This helped my mind to see that nothing lasts for forever. I would make it home after one of his weekends and be able to breathe and unclench my spirit from anxiety mode that seemed a constant.

The stark contrast in my two living spaces helped me understand that what was going on was the choices of those involved. Not necessarily how a particular "normal" was supposed to be. Once again, my mind was given what was necessary to realize that from the beginning I had choices to make about what was going on as well. I was determining what I would do with what was happening to me from the beginning.

Chapter 6

Childhood

"Have you seen my childhood? I'm searching for
the world that I came from 'cause I've been looking
around in the lost and found of my heart."

–*Michael Jackson*

I was a forty-year-old trapped in a little girl's body. I feel as
if I did not really have a childhood. Because of the beatings
she endured, my mother underwent several hospitalizations
throughout my elementary school years. They would happen
out of nowhere, and I would be thrust into the parent role for
our little family. My future stepfather did not live with us yet.
My mother would have a kidney stone attack, which would
require that she be taken to the hospital via ambulance. I was

left to take care of us kids until my grandmother could get to us by train or bus from Detroit.

This happened multiple times during my elementary school years. All of our neighbors were awesome humans, and we took care of each other. One couple were both police officers, and they would take me to the hospital to visit my mom so I could get checks signed to pay bills. When they had their first babies, twins named Mecca and Myra, I babysat for them for as long as we lived next to them.

I could not take money out of my mother's account to buy groceries. The store in our neighborhood in Lansing was owned by the most wonderful couple who lived in the back. Fabiano's did not have everything we needed, but it had enough. I could call the store and tell him what we needed, and he would give me a total and promised to take a check, since he knew my mother. I would ride my bike down there to pick up everything, and depending on how much I ordered, my brothers might have to be enlisted as well.

I learned how to do things that most adults choose not to master. At eleven, I was cooking meals that would have probably gotten me a show on the Cooking Channel. I got my brothers up for school and would run home to make lunch. I don't recall each of my mom's stints in the hospital being very long, but long enough to teach me the things adults did to keep a family going.

At this time, we were living in a house that my mother somehow managed to afford. It was a barn style that had two stories and a basement. My brothers and I lived in half of the upstairs in one large bedroom. My mom, and eventually our stepdad, had the other half.

My mother had been an accountant for a dress shop, and my stepfather was a skilled mechanic. They made the decision to create a combined business that allowed them to work out of our home and garage. This allowed us to have the stability of a parent at home all the time.

We would come home for lunch during this time, and my mother would invite all the kids in the neighborhood on occasion. Bread cost ten cents a loaf, and when she made French toast for lunch, it was like the Pied Piper had gone through several blocks surrounding our home.

Our chores were divided in a hybrid version of traditional roles. My brothers took out the garbage and cleaned up after the dog. I did most of the indoor chores. For the most part, I recall our years in this place as relatively calm. We did normal everyday things. We played in the streets until the lights came on and then headed home for dinner.

* * *

One weekend during the winter, we were getting ready to go Christmas shopping as a family. Everyone was getting dressed, and I had the additional chores of cleaning up the kitchen and doing the dishes. My parents' rule was that if we half-assed something, we would have to do everything over again. For me, this meant that if I did not do the dishes correctly, they ALL came out of the cupboards for me to do them again. As you can imagine this made me very meticulous.

We headed out to Meijer Thrifty Acres, Michigan's version of Walmart, and were gone until dark. Upon our return to our house, we walked in to discover a single coffee cup sitting on the dining table. My heart sank. I began my protest. I knew I had done every dish and dried and put them up. I would not have missed one cup. I could see my parents mulling over my logic, and it was late, so they gave me a pass until the next day when they would render my verdict. I have a photographic memory and knew something was not right. It did not make for a restful night.

We were all startled awake by the sounds of police cars and loud talking. We would come to find out that in the middle of the night our stepfather heard something in the basement and went to investigate. He was hit over the head and tied up. He saw his assailant. It was our father. All of this was outside the bounds of logic.

I seriously wanted everyone to acknowledge the coffee cup's origin. My logical defense mechanism was to focus on what was going to dictate my future and not the ridiculousness of what our father had done. I still do not know the outcome. We never spoke of it. Visitation with him did not pause.

* * *

It is funny how time moves when we are children. Feeling like slow motion during the school year and then the blink of an eye for summer vacation. I believe we were in this home for several years, and then another relocation was decided. We moved several times during my childhood, which resulted in different schools each time.

I was a smart kid and accelerated academically. I thrived on how school was taught back then, and there were several types of curricula that let you go at your own pace. I would blaze through them, and the teachers had to decide what to do with me after that. They chose to give me additional grades for being a tutor. I was an introverted extrovert even back then, but this was my logic space, and I thrived. My father's harsh treatment of me regarding intelligence or academic achievement just drove me harder.

We were now going to move yet again. This time to the lake property in Decatur, Michigan, where my maternal grandfather had already built a home to retire to with our grandmother. Our grandfather owned a good-size property that had a little dirt road running through it. We were going to be living in a single-wide trailer while a house was going to be built on the plot on the other side of the little dirt road.

I would be enrolled in junior high school at this time. Junior high has no vivid memories for me, good or bad. I was pretty good at the details, and this gap in time once again scares me for what may have happened between my memories.

This move made our visits with our father further apart, since we lived farther away now. None of us complained at this time, and my younger brother would cry to get out of going regularly.

On several of our visits, my father's wife would have the wounds of war that were all too recognizable. He would lie and say she was clumsy and fell down the stairs or something. I am not sure what our IQs were, but we were not dummies.

Our father's house was in Dearborn, in the "thumb" of Michigan. When we went with our father, the three of us kids stayed in one room which took up most of the top floor. I found myself lingering up there with my favorite books or even just enjoying the quiet. My brothers were always headed to the television and Saturday morning cartoons.

One morning, my father came into the room. He looked around as if to confirm we were the only two there. He walked over to my bed. Instead of sitting on the side, he sort of climbed on from the end and landed on top of me. I had the covers on, almost up to my neck. This did nothing to comfort me.

The terror is palpable even today. I was familiar with what was seemingly going to take place. I was shaking to the core. He was brushing my hair off my face. He had coffee breath. He was whispering about me being his girl. The weight of him made me feel trapped. I started whimpering. His annoyance showed up in his voice. Tears were streaming down my face.

Thankfully, this appeared to irritate him. For the first time in my life, I didn't mind that he chose to slap me. He told me to shut up. Then he got up and left the room. He did not try this again . . . at least not on me.

* * *

As we got older, we could think for ourselves . . . an inconvenient truth for an abuser.

Our visits became mechanical. The first night, typically a Friday, we would go eat somewhere fancy. My previous lessons had me on my best behavior. The conversation was generally about life stuff and how school was going.

There were no more Saturday morning visits to our bedroom to wake me up. We would either go to some event for the first half of the day on Saturday or just stay at our father's house until the usual evening festivities began.

At this point, every single weekend became a "Groundhog Day" for us. Family friends of our father were their drinking buddies every Saturday night. They had thirteen kids, some of whom were older, so we had built-in babysitters, and the adults would head out.

I actually enjoyed all the kids. Their home was raucous and fun, and, at the same time, peaceful. I did not have to walk on eggshells. I got to be a kid for a bit. One of their daughters was the poster child for multiple sclerosis and was one of the most delightful humans I had ever met. She was happy and did not want pity or an advantage. If we were playing a game, she was all in. The Lord grew me and my understanding of compassion and loving others.

We would be left at their house until the wee hours, and

on most occasions, we'd be falling asleep. The parents would finally get back. They reeked of cigarette smoke and were loud and obnoxious. My father would yell at us and herd us into the car to head home. I felt in my spirit the sadness of this particular goodbye to the kids, since I knew I had made up my mind for this time to be the last.

Physical

Chapter 7

Here Comes Life

"Let choice whisper in your ear and murmur in your
heart. Be ready. Here comes life."

–*Maya Angelou*

Turns out, the old wives' tale is true . . . climbing stairs induces
labor. It was August, and mom was craving strawberries. It
was the middle of the night, and they were in the fridge in
the kitchen. It was a two-story house and she had to do some
stair-climbing to get them. At 4 a.m. on August 8, 1962, at St
Joseph Hospital in Fort Wayne, Indiana, God made the intro-
ductions. "Shelly, here is your momma." "Matty, here's your
only baby girl, Shelly." He chose my momma because I would
need her strength, integrity, and grit.

The beatings began before my arrival and were taking place

while I was in the womb, so I had been moved around a bit. Breach . . . mooning the world that would soon reject me. At four and a half pounds, it was the only time in my life that I was under-weight. I was not obese at any time, just always the "chubby-cheeked" girl when I was little.

My memories are strong. Excuses were made by my father for each beating I received; however, I do not recall what I did to deserve them. The beating of my face for having lost a shoe when I was two probably left the most lasting physical damage to that side of my face. The entire left side of my face hemorrhaged and left me with a squint at the lower eye and cheek level. I refer to it as my "Clint Eastwood" squint.

As I grew up, it became clear that I was taking after my father's side of the family, genetically speaking. Our center of gravity was on the low side. My mother was 5'4" and never weighed over 100 pounds. She was an adopted only child, so I had no other family members for comparison on that side. I do look like my mother in my facial features, but from the neck down, I was all Vrabel.

Prior to our younger brother's arrival, my older brother Bob and I managed to get into mischief and entertain ourselves when the occasion called for it. Whether it was mischief or well-mannered frivolity, we were in it together. One summer night when I was two and my brother was three, our father had a backyard barbeque of some sort that brought only adults to our house. With no other children to keep us occupied, we were on our own to navigate the food, beverages, and anything else that seemed interesting.

People kept coming and going from our garage with glasses of liquid, and this seemed like a good place to start. We began our investigation, and it led to a large round can with a faucet.

Everyone was filling their glasses and exclaiming how good and cold it was. You did not need to ask us twice.

My brother dragged a milk crate underneath the faucet and helped me scramble up. We did not have any cups, so we figured straight into our mouths would do. I stood there on the crate, wearing only a diaper, and the frothy cold beverage was flowing down the length of me as I gulped. My brother got me down and took his turn.

Shortly after he finished, we both staggered into the breeze-way between the house and the garage. On our way to the backyard, I face-planted right then and there. We were later told that the beverage was beer, and that I was out for two days and my brother for four hours. Neither of us could hold our liquor then. A problem we would resolve later in life.

* * *

My maternal grandmother made most of my clothes, and this always included the frilly panties that covered my diaper. For the most part, I at least looked girly when I was little. They bought me dolls, doll houses, and buggies. I had more tea sets than you could count. My hair was always in little pigtails, and I was always in a dress.

When I was about three years old, my maternal grand-parents were visiting us at our house on Bluegrass Road. My brothers were staked out in the bedroom as the "main street" town. I was driving my buggy from the kitchen down the hall. My grandmother swooned, believing I was playing with dolls. She came over to me to discover I had a gun in the buggy, and I was heading to town to rob the bank. Apparently, having two brothers brought out a bit of the tomboy in me.

It was the '60s, and there were no rules about helmets or training wheels. We were told to play outside until someone called us for dinner. We flew headlong down the hill at the end of the street having bicycle races. We were allowed BB guns and ammo. It was a free-for-all.

We did not have the money to eat high on the hog. We ate the typical American diet at that time. Which was actually pretty close to whole foods, since there weren't a lot of processed foods back then. Genetically, I had a low center of gravity, but we were so active that I never crossed the line into truly overweight until later.

We are so wonderfully created that it is fascinating what our minds and bodies can go through and survive. Despite the damage inflicted by my father, my brothers and I were involved in some of the same childhood experiences as everyone else.

Riding bikes with the neighborhood kids until dark. Using our imaginations to create our own sports and games. Somehow, dirt managed to be a component of each one. Flying downhill on a bike, even though it had training wheels, we still flew headlong into the cornfield at the bottom of the hill. Surprisingly, I never broke anything and only got actual stitches playing softball much later.

My brothers and I got into mischief both together and in cahoots against one another. My younger brother, John, had a knack for causing my older brother and me to teach him life lessons. On one occasion, he had been particularly annoying. I am sure he did not do anything that any other younger brother does; however, he was ours and action was taken.

We decided to convince him we were playing hide-and-seek. We sat our younger brother on a stack of towels in the linen closet and closed the door. My older brother and I proceeded to go back to our bedroom and play or read. It was not normal for there to be long spans of quiet when the three of us were in the same room. Our mother noticed the void.

She came into the room and asked, "Where is your brother?"

Our mother had a philosophy with us that was true until we went out into the world on our own. She told us if we told the truth we would not get punished. On each occasion, we would make her reconfirm this covenant before spilling the beans.

"He's playing hide-and-seek," we chimed.

"With whom?" she asked.

A glance between us caused an impatient exhale, and we did not want to lose ground on the aforementioned promise. "He's in the linen closet."

I get the fact that I do not have a poker face from my mother. We had gotten on her last nerve with this one. She ran to the linen closet and flung it open.

My brother was sitting there quietly and shouted, "Boo, Momma!"

In our defense, the door had slats, so he was not deprived of oxygen or light. Not that our mother found comfort in that.

* * *

My older brother and I loved our younger brother and spent a lot of our childhood protecting him. I understand the irony of us "teaching" him, too. But siblings are allowed to do that. He would get into things that we knew would get him a beating from our father. So, we jumped in and tried to avert said beating. It didn't always work, and we didn't realize that our mother had the same plans for all of us. Our younger brother was exasperating, and it took a team of us to man the fort.

On one occasion, our little brother decided to investigate where the hamper chute in our parents' bathroom led to. I have never seen one anywhere else except in our childhood home. This hamper chute was in our parents' bathroom and led to the basement where the washer and dryer were. My mother had taught us to put our laundry down the chute, which was mildly entertaining.

Our little brother devised a plan to make it more sporting. After putting our father's white dress shirts down the chute, he opened the medicine cabinet and began a bombing run.

Shockingly, back then a lot of first aid ointments and medicines were loaded with food coloring. Typically, a disgusting kind of red-orange, and the smell was equal to the task. My older brother and I heard a kind of whistling, which did in fact sound like bombs dropping. We decided to investigate and to our horror found our little brother poking his head into the laundry chute to assure himself of his projectile hitting its mark.

We had no idea how many strafing runs he had made and were terrified to look. Upon closer examination, we discovered that the white dress shirts had made for a soft landing, but not soft enough to save all the bottles from breaking. All medicine bottles were glass back then, and at least one of them was Merthiolate, one of the particularly awful-smelling antiseptics for every kind of scratch, cut, or burn. It stung like nobody's business and was bright red-orange.

This was not going to end well. Before we could race to the basement to do anything, we ran into our mother in the hall. None of us was genetically gifted with a poker face, and our mother was no dummy. Two and two were put together. We spilled our guts and tried to protect our brother, but our mother ultimately took the blame. That was a loud night.

* * *

It was not that any of us did not do anything that was even worth a spanking. We did stuff kids do, and some of it deserved a spanking, or at least a stern lecture. Occasionally toys, TV, or treats were withheld. We just went on autopilot to protect one another, regardless of the consequences, and sometimes the outcome was unpredictable.

While we were all partners in crime, I did enjoy my inner world that kept me safe from adults and grown men in particular. I learned to read early on, and it opened up a whole world of fantasy for me that, in my mind, kept me safe and brought me joy.

My maternal grandmother got me any books I wanted. She was a voracious reader herself, and I think this was her version of parking the kids in front of the television in the '60s.

I loved the adventures my brothers and I had in the cornfields behind our house. We did not have a bunch of toys, but we had each other and our imaginations. We were outside, moving and creating. No one was concerned about body image at this time. Culturally, emphasis was on kids being healthy and growing appropriately.

My brothers and I never teased one another when we played, and I don't recall anyone at school having something to say, either. It did not matter to us. We were all kids, and we just figured out how to play together. For my brothers and me, at that house, it was survival. Time would come with teasing and bullying, but for now, we were circling the wagons.

For my fifth birthday, and before all hell broke loose between my parents, I got to have a cowboy-themed birthday party at this house on Bluegrass Road. I asked for a cowboy hat, guns with holsters, and cow-pattern chaps. All of which I received, much to my grandmother's chagrin. After everyone left and it was starting to get dark outside, I went to our driveway. We had floodlights that came on at dusk. I stood on one of the railroad ties by our driveway and practiced my quick draw while looking at my shadow. It is funny what we literally remember in the midst of things we would like to forget.

* * *

It was not long after this that we were surviving the chaos that would end our parents' marriage and move us to a new home and school. Our father was a successful professional, and when the divorce took place, we found ourselves in a new economic bracket. One that was receiving no support from him.

You could tell by our appearance we did not have a lot of money. We were not unclean or unkempt. Our mother would have had none of that. We just did not get a lot of new clothes or items for school. We had to wear things until we could not. We shared school supplies. Our mother repaired our clothes and cut our hair. She did a good job; it was just obvious we were frugal.

I was being sexually molested at this time and was terrified of everyone. It was at this stage in school that kids seemed to need to find a reason to make someone else the target of commentary, and if it kept them safe from friendly fire, everyone took a turn. If people called me names or told me I was fat or ugly . . . well, I just believed them. Not because I believed in my heart that these things were true about me. Because they said them out loud, like my father, I knew it was about them.

This did not stop the bruise from forming after every word hit its mark. It was more growing into someone who could see where the real wounds lie. It made me sad that perhaps that other kids, too, were having some of the same experiences in their house.

The apartment we lived in while the sexual abuse was happening was in a downtown area. It was small, and my brothers and I shared a room with bunkbeds. The only rooms I can picture were the bedroom and the living room. The trauma held me in its grip, and I weirdly recall that we had to cross a major thoroughfare on a footbridge overpass to a little neighborhood grocery store . . . where they had the candy. After school had me terrified and took up the space in my mind.

After the exposure and ending of the abuse, we moved to yet another elementary school in Okemos. We were not there for too long, and I did not have the time to develop a best friend or even after school playmates. It was not horrible, and I think I was just happy for no pain or chaos. However, it was at this school that the first dose of teasing became real. I was not morbidly obese, but definitely chubby. A fact other children would point out.

It was difficult to find outfits that were particularly feminine if you carried a few extra pounds. Up to this point in my life, it did not seem a primary concern about how I felt or if I liked what was happening around me. Clearly, including abuse, I did not feel the need to share what was happening to me or how I felt, and so, as a result, nothing changed.

In my mind, I can picture this particular house and several pleasant memories, at least within our family unit. Our visits with our father got a little further apart, and that was definitely better for my overall health. I continued my genetic journey looking like my father's side of the family, to my chagrin. They all tended to have more of a pear shape, and a hearty one at that. The fact that there was not junk food at that time and we played outside a lot probably kept something much worse at bay.

Rolling Stone

"If we were meant to stay in one place, we
would have roots instead of feet."

–*Rachel Wolchin*

The next house was a mixed bag of hard things, bizarre things, and normal life things. This is where I lost a lot of what was left of my childhood through the responsibilities I had to take on. My mother would have kidney stone attacks and have to be hospitalized. Sometimes just for a few days, other times for a couple weeks. Until my grandmother could get there on the train, we had to pick up the slack.

I got my first job at this time, a paper route. Actually, an assistant on a paper route for my older brother. My mother was an accountant and taught me to save some of my money. I put all the money I made into a Christmas Club account, which was a special kind of savings account for kids. It taught you how to save for "Christmas," so I was covered for giving gifts.

After a couple of tumultuous years at this house, with my mother's hospitalizations and the attack on my stepfather by my father, my mother and stepfather decided to create businesses that went together and worked out of our house. Staying in proximity to the house and us kids made for a little more stability. The economy at that time was not a friend to small business, and not having rent to pay was a blessing as well.

My mother was an accountant and made her office in the back mudroom of the house, and my stepfather was an automotive mechanic and utilized a huge garage we had in the back yard. After all the recent trauma, it was a comfort to see her face when we came home for lunch and when we got out of school.

I learned how to write checks so bills would not go unpaid when my mother was hospitalized. I helped my stepfather with grocery shopping and preparing meals for all of us. Our family laundry was done in the basement using a wringer washer. I helped my mother in her accounting business, which probably established the skill sets I use to this day.

Do not get me wrong; I did go to school and get to play. I just learned about and did adult things very early on. I understood the exhaustion of dropping on the bed after a long day. I could make a three-course home-cooked meal while doing my homework. I could balance a checkbook. For extra allowance, I cleaned carburetors for my stepfather and learned how to do oil changes.

My mother was very resourceful and had many skills. As did most women her age, since they had been taught how to cook, clean, sew, bake, and keep a home. On one particularly creative occasion, my mother decided to make clothes for us to save money. She knew how to sew well and had worked at a dress shop prior to marrying our stepfather, so she had a sense of fashion. The clothes were very well-made, and most of the patterns were not awful. Until she made us matching outfits.

The fabric looked like its original destination should have been curtains. She made us white dress shirts to wear with the ensemble of a vest and a pair of bellbottoms. Identical. We were forced to wear them . . . on the same day . . . to school. We looked like the Partridge family, minus the talent. As if being overweight and wearing ridiculously thick glasses was not enough to make me a target, I now had a matching outfit with my brothers that looked like upholstery. Good grief.

* * *

While in elementary school, I grew to my full height of 5'7". I wasn't obese but did have more weight than I should for my height. My best friend Don and his dozen older brothers taught me how to be good at sports and use how I was built to my advantage. They never made me feel like anything was wrong with me, and while they were awesome, we did not think about "liking" each other back then. I cannot imagine that my mind or heart could have handled any version of that. We simply enjoyed competing together and surviving elementary and middle school.

At school, Don and I were always the captains who got to choose teams. It was a bit of a bummer, since I would have liked to be on his team and vice versa. Because I got my height early, I excelled at sports, and a couple in particular. Softball and hockey were the early favorites. I was built for both. My low center of gravity made me a good catcher in softball. In hockey, Don's brothers had taught me how to use my body as a goalie. I mean, as long as it takes up a fair bit of space, may as well use it wisely.

In the Midwest, there were certain activities as a family that took place during each season. Bowling in the winter and drive-in movies in the summer. I took to bowling like a fish to water. I was tall and sturdy for a fifth grader and could throw a ten-pound bowling ball like an adult. No one bowled "just for fun." You were generally corralled into a league that played weekly.

My stepfather and mother were in a couples league sponsored by their business and were happy that I enjoyed bowling and loved taking me to events. In one tournament, I bowled a 260 (300 is a perfect game in bowling), and my stepfather was so proud he bought me my own bowling ball with my initials engraved on it, along with a bag and shoes. It was something I was good at and not hindered by my weight. I loved my time bowling, since it was the first time I seemed to get positive attention and praise for something I was accomplishing on my own.

* * *

I was accelerating in academics at this time as well and was made a mentor to kids a couple of years older than me who needed the help. This brought on the bullying of being a nerd. Several of the students I was actually helping began to bully me. They would follow me home and harass me the entire way.

My mother was not into violence, and I was not a fan of people who hit, either. However, my stepfather was a Golden Gloves boxer and decided I needed to protect and defend myself. So, he taught me a few things. The first of which was that, generally speaking, if you stand up for yourself, people will be scared off. Secondly, he taught me how to be a really good boxer and recruited my brothers and other kids in the neighborhood to be my sparring partners.

On the first occasion I got to employ his particular tactics, I was heading home from school one afternoon. A girl who was in the middle of the pack of thirteen siblings followed me home and got them all to join her and to harangue me along the way.

I simply kept walking for the first couple blocks. Their verbal abuse was not getting the reaction they had hoped for, so they decided to surround me and block my way. We were on a corner at the bottom of a hill where I was to take a left toward home and the route to their home would have taken them forward. The home on the corner had a large yard that was almost entirely a garden. The older gentleman who lived there was watering plants and watching the scenario develop.

The imminent threat of something physical was having an impact on me that was not visible to the naked eye. I knew what being yelled at felt like. That wound was still open. I understood the feeling of a fist colliding with my face. That wound had not completely healed. My mind was working feverishly to avoid tearing at either of them.

The crowd of kids had gotten pretty big at this point. I was not confident that anyone would help me or come to my rescue, including my brothers, so I had to devise a plan. I knew if I had to, I could fight the girl, but there were thirteen of them, and I didn't know if they would fight fair.

As with my father's taunting before he would beat me as a child, there would come a moment where I wanted them to either shut up or hit me.

Since fighting all of them was out of the question, I decided to sit down and started screaming. My brothers were on the fringes of the large group that had formed, and even they were caught off guard. Several of the thirteen started toward me, and my screaming got louder. It did not take long for them to all freak out and leave. As my brothers reached to help me up, the older gentleman came over and told me that my tactics were genius. Genius or not, those particular kids never tried it again.

I determined at a young age that whether I knew what I was doing or not, I was not going to be beaten or abused again. Later in life, standing 5'7" tall would not be substantial, but for elementary and middle school, it would be enough to see this stand through.

* * *

It felt like being in the witness protection program. We moved every couple of years, and no one knew who we were. It took everything I had to start over. I would have preferred to stay home and read my books. At least in that world there were tidy endings.

It usually felt like a sudden move, but that was probably "kid" timing. We were just suddenly living somewhere else. No discussion, the packing and the moving all a blur of no remembrance.

We moved west across the state to a property in Decatur that my maternal grandfather had acquired to build a retirement home for himself and my grandmother. Our new home this time was a single-wide trailer on the plot across the street.

I suffered physical and sexual abuse from birth to six years of age. This created an impact on me hormonally and really started the ball rolling with my shape and health. I was always that chubby-cheeked little girl and could not shake that moniker through elementary school, and the nicknames got worse heading into middle school.

During this time, we were being forced to go on visitation with my biological father, and this wreaked havoc on my emotions and physical condition. If the people who are supposed to love you do not think very highly of you . . . why should you? I did not have low self-esteem; I simply did not think about myself much.

I had always been called "big-boned," and I am not sure why anyone thought that was a good synonym for fat. Since I was an emotional eater at that time, all of the chaos did loads to make matters worse. I even became covert about it. I look back and feel I could be a part of the CIA or something for my ability to cover my tracks. However, it was painfully obvious that I was physically changing in accordance with my habits. I was carrying weight I did not want, and since I did not talk to anyone about anything, nothing changed.

While there wasn't a plethora of diet and nutrition plans back then, there was my parents philosophy of "get off your butt and go outside," so I would go outside and practice whatever sport season was coming up. My weight wasn't fatal, and it did not deter my sports capabilities. I believe this was because we did not have electronics or even multiple television channels to make "couch potatoes" of us. We went outside and played until we were exhausted, and this helped keep my pathetic metabolism from running the show.

Except for gym class, there wasn't any availability of club sports during those couple years. I had my full height in junior high and double-D-cup boobies, which gathered another kind of attention. My center of gravity did make me a great setter in volleyball, and both pitching and catching in softball seemed more suited to my genetics.

I blossomed under my coaches in Michigan but was having the same family and visitation issues the whole time. When I was fourteen and decided to take a stand and end our visitations, I had a rush of relief and a reduction in stress. However,

I now had the full force of rejection by my father, and that was not easy to swallow.

Every single thing he had ever shouted at me. Every single thing he had said I would become without him. This would be my time to prove that everything I would become had everything to do with how I was created to survive and how my Jesus showed me the way.

Being rejected by those who were supposed to love me became a theme for both my physical and emotional well-being. When I was younger, I was an emotional- and stress-eater. Ironically, later in life, I became the opposite. During junior high and high school, I received attention from boys . . . and men . . . that was unhealthy and toxic. I did not avoid it because I was smart and discerning. I avoided it because I was scared to death.

Season II

WONDER YEARS

Chapter 9

Outsiders

> "You get tough like me and you don't get hurt. You
> look out for yourself and nothin' can touch you . . ."
>
> *–The Outsiders*

There I was, all alone, like a cow staring at a new gate. Wearing my vulnerability body spray and looking like I did not belong anywhere. Easy prey for those with no good intentions.

When I started high school, I was initially chosen by a group of outsiders. While I was a geek and did play sports, so many things about me kept those groups from being a fit for me. I guess I just really didn't fit in anywhere. I didn't know who I really was and had been hiding and protecting my heart so much that even I didn't know what I might do next.

They saw me surviving by myself. It was like a scene from *The Outsiders*. The Greasers and Socs at their designated tables in the cafeteria. Even though I was a jock, I was an awkward new kid and was invisible unless you needed more gang members. The one thing the outsiders knew I needed was to belong. It was what brought them together as well.

They smoked on the corner just off school property, wearing their uniform of white T-shirts with the sleeves rolled up and beat-up jeans. Decatur was a one-stoplight town, and the sum total of the commerce was mainly down Phelps Street. A little mom-and-pop convenience store was just a short walk from the school. The gang would head for the store, going up and down the aisles in small groups. Some members would steal while they convinced the members of the gang that had some money to buy things in order to distract the owners. I did not know this protocol and was the perfect patsy. I realized they didn't have money and thought I was merely being used to get them snacks. The fact that they liked me for it was okay with me.

On one occasion, we were halfway back to the school when there was a lot of yelling and running moving quickly in our direction. Threats of police and expulsion scared the life out of me. My mother was not to be trifled with. Jail would have paled in comparison with what she would have done.

The owner caught up to the slower-moving members of the herd, that would include me, and retrieved the stolen items. He informed the thieves that they were not welcome in his store again. He acknowledged that I was not a criminal and that I should choose my friends more wisely. This was the first step to my exit from the outsiders.

Mind you, my time with them was probably only a few weeks, since my sports schedule didn't have space for smoking and loitering. At no time did I feel particularly comfortable about my place in this particular group. I felt like Sandra Dee in the Pink Ladies in *Grease*. I did not steal anything but was merely unwittingly used as the stooge decoy. I did not partake in the pinched goods and only took a small amount of berating for it. I do not doubt that they knew all along I was a poser.

The sum total of my smoking was puffing with no inhaling and probably turning green in-between puffs. To be honest, I never really liked smoking. My mom and my stepfather, and, well, frankly, all adults smoked back then, and I thought it was truthfully disgusting. The fact that everyone was doing it made it seem less degenerate than it was, and so I was more easily persuaded to go along.

Based on what some of the couples in the group were willing to do out in the open, sexual relations were definitely part of the bylaws. This is when my devotion to the outsiders found its boundary. I may have gone on in life to choose the wrong men for my heart, but I was definitely not going to let anyone sexually abuse me ever again.

* * *

I now transitioned over to the geeky, jock part of my journey. More geek than jock, but still a 180 from the wrong crowd. The geek moniker was a good fit because I was maniacal about doing well in school. The jury was out on whether or not I was a jock. I loved sports, and if the past was representative, I was bound to do well at something in high school. However, the title "jock" generally came with an overall look and performance, so I don't believe that is how I am remembered.

I was built for comfort, not for speed, and found my lane in both softball and volleyball. I had zero confidence that I would be accepted by the other girls going into the tryouts, as I was a newcomer and had some proving to do. Volleyball was the sport closest to the beginning of the school year and was my first courageous attempt to fit in.

I had never even seen a volleyball prior to this tryout. Despite being bottom-heavy, I took to it like a fish to water. I was built for setting and defense and made the starting team, a team that would go on to state championships during my time.

While there was not a plethora of advanced classes or electives back in my day, there were enough options to keep me from being bored. High school homework was robust and actually taught us things that would be beneficial for real life. With the possible exception of algebra. Why were we adding letters anyway?

I loved learning. My mother said I was born asking, "Why?" Decatur had a small school system, and it became apparent quickly who the "geeky" kids were. We all gravitated toward one another when group projects were required, since we knew all involved would participate and pull their weight. We had healthy competitiveness regarding placement in the "Top Ten" academically, and that, coupled with my natural bent toward "why?" helped me stay sharp.

I joke that I was suicidal in school if I got an A-. This was not far from the truth. Academic excellence was a major incentive of mine until well after high school. I was fortunate to have a photographic and phonographic memory, which made striving for that perfection much easier. But I did fall short here and there, and it took its toll. I would begin to go down the rabbit hole of believing my father may have been right when he said I would not have success academically without him in my life. This would devastate me and definitely bring on some low-level depression.

* * *

It was during this time that I met my best friend, Bethany. This precious soul came out of a sea of humanity and loved me unconditionally. We could not have been more opposite in regard to almost everything. Perhaps our differences are the exact reason why we were the best fit for each other.

Bethany wore these frilly white blouses with embroidery on the Peter Pan collars and a chain that held her glasses like a little old lady. I giggle as I type this, picturing her, the very image of femininity, while I was a tomboy and wore jeans and T-shirts and had no girly presence about me whatsoever.

I was called upon often to answer questions, more an attempt to make up for the lack of participation by the class rather than my desire to be front and center. Bethany, on the other hand, raised her hand incessantly followed by, "I have a question" to the point where we all chimed in with her. I adored her, and we embraced one another and our stuff.

She invited me to her church the first day we met. Church opened up a can of worms for me after how we had been treated by the priest after my mother's divorce, so it was a while before I took her up on the offer. My Bethany softened me up. She was not tough by the world standards, but she was compassionate and kind. She was what I needed, and the Lord knew it. He took care of her, too. She did not need to be tough because He had her covered.

Decatur was extremely rural and agricultural. Bethany's family had a pig farm located near all the other farms. Our home was on a lake near woods and a campground. We did not live near one another and therefore only got to see one another at school in the beginning of our friendship.

From the very first sleepover, Bethany and her family were a fit for me. I could see where Bethany got her kind, sweet spirit. They embraced me like family and never looked back. They loved me well. Some of my favorite times in life were spent with her and her family at their house.

They sat down at the table for dinner every night. The whole family. No exceptions. I got to see firsthand a biblical portrait of a marriage and a family. How God intended couples and families to value and treat one another. They were not perfect. But they were humble, hardworking, and kind. They loved me and prayed for me and always made me feel welcome in their home.

Her mother taught me how to make divinity, and we were all better for it. I mean, seriously: divinity is like crack. Heavenly pillows of delight. But good gravy, Marie, did it take time and elbow grease to make. Bethany's momma did not have a KitchenAid or a stand mixer. We had to mix it with a handheld mixer. We would pour a hot mixture of sugar, corn syrup, and water over beaten-stiff egg whites, and then we were off to the races. We had to beat it until just the right glossiness and then put in finely chopped nuts of choice and then . . . heaven. Her momma swore I was the only one who got it divinely right. I remember those divinity afternoons as a sweet time with the three of us in the kitchen, gabbing away and just fun.

* * *

Bethany and I went to each other's everything. She to my sports tryouts. Me to her band or cheerleading. We accepted each other's diverse interests and supported one another. Bethany's first cheerleading tryouts were coming up and she was beginning to feel skittish. She decided that a buddy would calm her fears. I assured her I would be present throughout the process. This was not what she had in mind.

She did not want to be in front of everyone alone. I could see where this was going, and I did not like it one bit. She begged. I kept envisioning myself in the little skirt. As if being big-boned, wearing thick glasses, and having the fashion sense of an orangutan wasn't enough, now my Bethany wanted me to get up and gyrate and cheer in front of a crowd. To which she replied, "Don't worry. You won't be alone. You'll have me there." She begged some more, and I finally relented. I immediately regretted it, but I had given my word.

The good news was that the entire tryout could not be with another person. Also, the committee was more than happy to not make me do anything else but represent for Bethany. I was mortified but survived and did not totally embarrass my best friend. What happened next, however, left an impression that I would imagine lives to this day.

My precious friend was doing great. She did appear to be counting like one would when taking steps in a dance routine. She looked adorable as she was completing the compulsory tricks. It all culminated in quite a flourish which ended with the splits. She had had trouble in practice going all the way to the floor in the sideways splits. The force of the finish accomplished the splits with a loud pop. Her hips had become disjointed, and she could not move or get up. I know medical professionals were called, but I did not believe an ambulance was ordered. Bethany did not find the humor for some time. She did come around when she found out she made the squad. I, sadly, was not invited to join.

* * *

After my first gym class with Bethany, the thought never occurred to me to ask her to try out for any sport. It was my comfort zone, and I didn't require a buddy for tryouts. Bethany was in the bleachers for every volleyball match and softball game that her family allowed her to attend. I went to all the games to support her cheerleading and usually got a sleepover out of it afterward as well.

Bethany's supportive heart got truly tested on one bizarre day in gym class. I had gotten the attention of some of the new members of the outsiders. Some of the kids who had been momentary friends during the street corner days did not like me thinking for myself and doing my own thing. They decided to have a couple of the bigger girls come teach me a lesson. They chose gym class as I was coming back to my locker from the showers, perhaps thinking if I was naked I would be more vulnerable.

It was like some sort of rumble out of *Happy Days*. I suddenly realized that there was no one else near me and that they were even kind of pressing up against the wall and parting to let someone through. Only Bethany was next to me, and she was fully dressed. She was so sweet and modest; I think she showered that way.

As the two girls rounded the row of lockers, I recognized the girl who tried to groom me, and the other one was new and bigger. Not a word had been said yet, and Bethany had pulled a Houdini act to put herself inside her locker. So, I was on my own. Not that I thought otherwise.

As they approached, I stood up, wearing only undergarments. The big one was about a foot from my face, and we were actually the same height. She leaned in to start speaking, and when I did not budge, it threw her off. She looked back at her friend and then turned to me again and barked her threat. I learned later that the gym teacher, who was also my volleyball coach, was at the end of the lockers and gave me a couple beats to respond.

The girl said, "You needed to get permission to leave the group. You are going to meet me after school, out back by the greenhouse to beat you up and teach you a lesson."

I found this incredibly comical that anyone would think

that someone would actually show up for a beating. However, it did seem to happen in the movies.

Having had my stepfather teach me how to box and stand up for myself, as well as other incidents in elementary school, prepared me to take a stand. Not to mention the fear of God my mother struck in me. I made my rebuttal. "I cannot meet you after school and miss my bus. My mother would kill me, and she scares me more than you. So, if you want to fight, let's go, right here, right now." I then took a step toward them, and they stumbled back and fell over one another. As they got up, the big one said, "You're nuts." Not sure she was wrong.

Bethany climbed out of the locker looking like she was going to faint. My coach came around the corner laughing and told me to get my butt moving to class. Beyond passing in the hall, I did not have any further encounters with any of the "old gang."

* * *

Bethany and her family saw the wear and tear having to go on visits with my father was having on me. They would have taken me to their house for sleepovers every weekend if her father didn't intercede. He loved having me there but knew as the leader of his family that I needed to be with my family as well.

Bethany and her mom would love on me by inviting me into their home and to church. I finally realized that what they had as a family came from the things they did as a family, and one thing that seemed important was going to church together. I did not realize then that it was more about what happened there, but that would come later. I agreed to join them, and you would have thought they had won some sort of sweepstakes by the response.

This chipped away at my walls and allowed Bethany and

her family to get a little closer. I may have been in their home dozens of times, and Bethany may have been present for my "rumble in the jungle," but that did not fully equate to trust yet. I was selective in what I shared. They knew my parents were divorced and that I had to spend every other weekend with my father, but they knew nothing beyond that.

My current wounds from those who were supposed to be trusted were still gaping, and the learning curve for my discernment had not been completed. Spending time with Bethany and her family was like a balm for my heart, and they had definitely opened me up more than anyone previously.

Chapter 10

Circle of Trust

"Many people will walk in and out of your life, but
only true friends will leave footprints in your heart."

—*Eleanor Roosevelt*

After going with Bethany and her family to church a few
times, my brothers asked to go as well. It turned out many
of their friends went there, and my brothers saw the opportunity to hang out. My grandfather agreed to take us every
Sunday morning. I think he felt that since we were products of
a broken family and that being at any church was better than
being left to our own devices. The church had many activities
and Sunday School for the high school kids. It kept us all doing
"wholesome" activities and offered alternatives to the school
dances.

My first normal feelings for the opposite sex came as a
by-product of being Bethany's sidekick. She fell madly in love

with a young man named Paul, who was in our youth group. At this time in our society, there was a higher moral standard when it came to dating. At least there was a more visible line of demarcation regarding those who had a standard and those who did not.

None of our parents would allow us to go on a date without a chaperone. So, I was there for Bethany and Steve stood in as chaperone for Paul. Now I wanted to crawl into a locker. Bethany and Paul tried their darndest to put Steve and me together, but it was seriously not meant to be.

To be fair, I was not very girly, and I was also terrified at the thought of a male being anything more than a friend. My heart was still pretty fragile. It did not stop us from having fun, though. It was nice and felt normal to engage with guys and not have our friendship become sexual or weird. We were weird enough already as teenagers. This became another time in my life that felt like a normal, relatively safe space.

No one in my closest circle had showed signs of making choices that would hurt me. Signs I had been taught to observe as I passed through each experience. At the very least, my heart did not feel anxious or the need to stay on guard all the time. Not with them, anyway.

* * *

Bethany did not have to do a thing to have Paul's undivided attention. They were made for each other from the start. She was, however, a handful with antics I believe she felt were entertaining. The part where the rest of us had to pick up after her was where the shine went off the apple for me.

Our church had a summer camping and canoeing trip every year for the high school kids. Now, canoeing is not rocket science. However, you do need some strength to paddle and navigate, especially rapids, and some common sense regarding the reality of rapidly moving water and rocks. My Bethany and I, of course, ended up in a canoe together. They all were two-man vessels. Bless her heart, she behaved as though it was some sort of nature ride that she could just sit back and enjoy. She acted all flighty but in retrospect had a perfect plan to keep Paul's favor.

They launched the canoes a couple at a time and then moments later the next two, and so on. She pestered me to get our canoe ready to go before Paul and Steve's. It was not until we were about halfway through the day's length of river that I became aware of her sneaky schemes.

There were a lot of beautiful willow trees that hung out over the water along the banks of the river. We were going to be coming up on some rapids, and the water was starting to move, when unbeknownst to me, Bethany reached up, grabbed a willow branch, and capsized us. We went under. The water was deep but crystal clear, and you could see the river bottom.

I wore glasses, and they came off and thankfully sank for me to find shortly. Our cushions and oars were another matter. I came up out of the water to watch them enter the rapids. Our canoe caught onto a large log, and we could not free it, although I use the word "we" loosely.

I looked over at Bethany to see her light up like a Christmas tree. Who was coming around the bend behind us but Paul and Steve? Paul beaming and ready to be her hero. Steve's face I can only imagine was mirroring mine. They got our canoe free and agreed that we would all hang on to each other's canoe to make it the short trip to base camp. We retrieved said cushions and oars on the way. Of all the wonderful traits my Bethany had, she was definitely not boring.

* * *

At fourteen years old, at a revival at our church in Michigan, I accepted Christ as my Savior. My best friend Bethany and her mother made a full-time job out of praying for me and loving on me. I cannot overstate what a galactically important moment in time this was for me. I did not go on to be perfect, in fact far from it, but this relationship with Christ would provide the tethers that kept me from floating too far from the foundation of truth.

It is, however, important to note this relationship for the sake of my emotional underpinnings. For two more years I was ensconced in the youth group at church and my role as Bethany's chaperone. Once again, there was Jesus shoring up connections with relationships that were not there to take advantage. Not there to hurt or reject.

No one in my youth group knew the specifics of what I had been through in my short life. They genuinely treated me in a way that expressed kindness and care for me as a sister in Christ. A member of the family as Jesus intended it to be, not as I had experienced family in my childhood.

My pursuit of excellence in academics brought me great joy, even if it later became a little unhealthy. I excelled at softball and volleyball and found another place where I did not have to have my guard up constantly. It was as if my coaches knew what I needed to have normal in my life. We were state champions in both sports, and as a team member, that was just the shot in the arm I needed.

A lot was going on at home, and we were weathering some of the worst winters Michigan had ever seen. My parents and grandparents made the decision to move to a better climate without so much as a by-your-leave. Mind you, as a non-income-producing member of our clan, I did not deserve a say, and that is how it was done then. Kids' thoughts on the matter were not taken into consideration.

The winter of 1977 was horrific. We loved it as kids because the snow days out of school were tallying up to over a month. But it got scary in regard to getting out to get food and electricity managing to stay connected. My mother had a seventy-two-mile round-trip commute to her job in Kalamazoo, and the winters were taking a toll on her mental and physical health. Something was going to have to give.

Unfortunately, the adults made the call, and we were going to follow our grandparents to Arizona. I was devastated. My place in the world felt relatively safe for the first time in my short life. Now they were going to make me start over.

We had the blueprints of the house we were having built in Decatur, on the lake, on the wall of our trailer. We had gotten to pick our bedrooms on the second floor. We were not visiting our father anymore, and so this was supposed to be home. I wanted no part in this move.

Bethany and her family were devastated also. The decision had been made in January, and the move was going to take place in the summer. I was going to finish my drivers ed class by the end of June, and we would then head out. My grandparents would be going out earlier, and we would meet up with them and then find a house.

Bethany had me over for a sleepover where we all cried. Her family offered to let me live with them to finish my last two years of high school. Her father was very kind and said that he would not let Bethany do the same but wanted me to know he was happy to allow me to be part of their family if my mother agreed.

Mom's answer was a no. No real explanation, just not staying in Michigan. I thought staying in Michigan with

Bethany was what I wanted, but I was the obedient child and the rule-follower, so I did not fight the move. I was completely heartbroken.

I spent as much time as was allowed hanging out with Bethany before the time came. There were not many people in the world at that time who said they loved me and meant it. I did not want there to be one less going with me to a strange world. We did not get to talk about the details of the move. Part of my heart was being left behind, and Bethany and I spent our time enjoying one another's company.

We had a bit of a "goodbye" tour, visiting some family before we left the state of Michigan. My stepfather's parents lived in Cadillac, and we drove up there to say goodbye. Even though it was eight years after the abuse, I am not sure why anyone in the family thought inviting my abuser to the family outing was a good idea. He showed up with his wife and son, and everyone acted like it was perfectly fine.

I had not seen him since his beating. He looked the same. I was trembling and felt like I would vomit the entire time. No one asked me if I was okay with him being there. It was as if they did not remember. Was something wrong with me because I did?

That particular wound was taking its time healing. I believe I needed to remember to understand that I did nothing wrong and so that I could understand how our choices affect ourselves and others. I would need this understanding to show myself grace for my own choices to come.

It was getting late, and we were going to be hitting the road early the next morning. So, everyone was gathering around crying and hugging. He and his wife and son stood there as my mother and stepfather said goodbyes and then informed us kids to do the same.

I began to tremble harder to the point of shaking. Tears were running down my face, but no sound was coming out. I could not move. My stepfather looked stricken and told me to go get into the RV. That was it. No one ever checked on me or asked if I was all right.

I understood what he had done to me at five years of age. My Jesus gave me the ability to reason out that it was nothing I had done and all a matter of this man's evil choices. Clearly, the wound had some healing to do, and this encounter did not help.

* * *

My maternal grandparents sold their retirement home and moved to Arizona before us. We had acquired an RV and made a family vacation out of moving to Arizona. After we said the family goodbyes and we got underway, the travel started to have a routine about it.

We got into a rhythm in tight quarters and were able to stop at KOA Campgrounds along the way to allow for a larger bathroom and shower to manage the claustrophobia. My stepfather had started long-haul trucking at that time and had our stops planned all the way to Arizona. My mother sprinkled in some historical and just plain fun stuff as well. I was in my reading fantasy world when we were driving, and that began to allow me to breathe normally again for a bit.

Until another opportunity presented itself for an older male to try to push himself on me. We made many stops at various tourist sites and family friends' homes along the way to Arizona. A friend of my mom's asked us to stay for a couple days with her and her new boyfriend. I am not sure how old they were but around my mom's age and that would have been in their late 30s.

They were all going to go to the store to get stuff for a BBQ, and I was on my period and felt like lying down and reading in our RV. Unbeknownst to me, the boyfriend had decided to stay back as well. He came and knocked on the RV door and came in to "chat." He started off on the couch talking about life in general. He was the perfect groomer. He showed interest in a vulnerable, abused young lady. He kept slowly shifting positions until he was sitting on the bed I had been lying on. I was familiar with this behavior in an abuser from both my stepfather's brother and my biological father who had attempted the same type of sexual abuse.

He started touching me and moving closer. I shifted position until my back was up against the wall. I pushed his hands off me, which caused him to be more aggressive. There was no one to save me.

To say I was panicking was an understatement. He moved closer and his touching was moving up my body and he was more persistent. I asked him to stop and began to cry. He appeared to take this as motivation. He got to the point where he was leaning in to kiss me when the group got back from shopping.

I was sobbing and heartbroken. He threatened me and told me that he would say I was lying and hurt me if I said a word. I was familiar with this brand of manipulation and abuse. I never said a word. I spent the next two days stuck to my brothers like glue.

Here I was, outside of my safe space that I had left behind in Michigan. Why was this happening again? Was I doing something to provoke this behavior in these men?

My Comforter showed me that not only was this the choice of this man, but that I now had the discernment to see it coming. I am not sure that I physically would have known what to do to stop him. But my reaction and the timing of the family return-ing showed me that I had been divinely protected with an out that I do not believe was coincidence.

Chapter 11

Walk by Faith

"For we walk by faith, not by sight."

(2 Corinthians 5:7)

It sent a shudder through the bowels of hell and a standing ovation in Heaven. My salvation let the world know . . . the whole world . . . who was my King.

I had no delusions that my life would now be puppies and rainbows. I did not believe that everything that happened to me would now be erased, although I hoped. In fact, that was the hard work that was about to begin. Reconciling all that had happened to me with my understanding of the choice we all had to follow Jesus.

The night I got saved, at a revival at our church, I came home to my family overly ecstatic to let them know the "good news." Someone, my King, was saying He loved me, and He meant it. I was fourteen, and since no one in my world had really talked to me about Jesus, I assumed they would all be grateful to hear of my conversion. Nothing could have been further from the truth.

My mother was not angry, but she wasn't pleased. I had been christened when I was a baby, and she felt I needed no "conversion" or to be born again. Within the Catholic church, which she had attended all her life, the study of the Bible was not left up to the parishioners. They attended catechism and got the basic tenets down. They attended church every Sunday and got any scripture reading from the priest along with communion. You made confession through an earthly representative and got your penance. What else did I require? I chose the tack of expressing to her what it really meant and the scriptures to back it up. This is where her patience ended.

She informed me that she did not accept any of this nonsense, and I was not allowed to follow my savior in believers' baptism, either. She told me at first that I would not be allowed to attend my church as well. This all was a body blow I had not anticipated in my wildest imaginations. After all, her church threw us out when she divorced my father.

I wisely, and probably by God's intervention, did not bring this up at this point in our conversation. Something, the Holy Spirit, gave me a peace about shutting up and honoring my mother's feelings on the matter. That I was okay because my relationship with Jesus was between Him and me, and it was going to be okay.

Because my grandfather had been taking my brothers and me to church every Sunday, with my grandmother's blessing, I decided to take my enthusiasm across the street. My grandparents were Lutheran, and while not as affronted as my mother, they also did not see the need for salvation. However, my grandmother knew that there were worse things teenagers could be doing than going to church, so she did not forbid my grandfather from taking us. A decision that did not please my mother, but she did not debate the matter further.

My happiness being dashed, I decided to reach out to Bethany and her family. She had me over for a sleepover to commiserate. Divinity covers a multitude of sins. See what I did there?

Bethany and her family listened to my plight and then gave it to me straight. First of all, I was to honor my mother. Period. Secondly, they told me about what my salvation had meant in heaven, and in hell. War was just beginning, and I needed to get prepared.

Bethany's dad was such a godly, patient man, and he let me know that my choices have consequences, good and bad, and that I needed to be careful not to give Satan a foothold. He did not know my whole story, but he knew I had been abused and that this was an opening Satan would exploit. I needed to be careful about overreacting and also about what I consumed. Every time I was in their home, they all helped me understand how to study, listen to, and be obedient to the Word of God.

Being born again meant starting over. I needed to start my journey off with the basics of understanding my relationship with Jesus. How to read the Bible. How to listen to the Holy Spirit regarding the meaning of the Word and application for my life. How to pray. How to walk daily in obedience to His purpose for me.

My brothers had gotten saved at the same revival as me; however, they did not share my enthusiasm out of the gate. I felt alone in my faith, and it was a little scary. I felt I had let myself be vulnerable and raw, and I had no one to share this with. Even though it was awesome . . . it felt the same as the other secrets I bore.

* * *

Back then, the only resources for a new believer were your church, church family, the radio, and television. I devoured what I could and probably drove Bethany's dad and my youth pastor crazy. There were times when I took the prevailing wisdom overboard.

One Saturday, I had listened to a particularly "fire and brimstone" sermon on the radio and took what the preacher had to say to heart. Interestingly enough, the sermon at church the next day had similar subject matter that I combined with the Saturday sermon and took to the extreme and out of context.

Both messages were discussing what we allow into our "ear and eye" gates. Kind of "you are what you eat" messaging. They spoke about actually hearing what the television shows and the music we listen to were really saying. How our brains take these words to heart and cause us to react accordingly. It was another form of temptation, and it was being crafted in a way that did not make it seem so bad.

So, I was fourteen, a brand-new believer, and these were adult believers that I figured knew more than me. Now, I am not saying they said or did anything wrong. I absolutely took what they said literally and developed an action plan from there. I did not seek wise counsel or pray about any of it. I just decided what was wrong with my lifestyle and leaped.

I belonged to the Columbia House mail order club. At that time, it was 8-tracks, but it eventually progressed to regular cassettes as well. You started out getting six for free with a bonus one for one cent. All you did was pay shipping. But then, they got you because you had to buy a certain number of additional cassettes over the next year, or they could charge you for the six that were free. I had been a member for a couple of years and had a lovely 8-track collection. Elvis, the Beach Boys, Barry Manilow, lots of Motown artists, etc . . .

Back then, you got an insert with the lyrics for the cassettes you bought, and so I could see in black-and-white what I was consuming. It truthfully had never occurred to me that anything was wrong with the music I was listening to. It just sounded good to me, and I liked singing and dancing along with it. Don't get me started on the prevailing wisdom of the morality of dancing.

Well, here comes my *Footloose* moment. I heard another radio message, and I was going straight to hell. Not only was the music I was listening to the music of the devil, but I had gone to several school dances to boot. Mind you, I was horrified of the males of my species and never actually danced, but nonetheless, I actually attended. And actually dressed to suit the occasion as well. Now, I was not built for provocative dancewear, so my wardrobe did not require the assault the rest of my life was about to receive.

I decided my family needed to see my public declaration of my sin being laid waste and grabbed all of my wretched cassettes and threw them into a bonfire I had started for dramatic affect. I informed them all that they should repent and do the same. I cannot imagine how I must have looked. Probably like Cruella De Vil from *101 Dalmatians* standing there, disheveled and ranting. It was quite the spectacle.

There was no way on earth my brothers would throw away the hard-earned cash that bought their cassettes. We had gone to the mattresses over many a situation, but this one had them ganging up on me.

My mother was not loud when she spoke. She was, however,

not to be ignored when she did. I believe my mother actually laughed at me. My mother had attended American Bandstand as a teenager in high school, and Elvis was the guest. An additional irony was that at this time in her life she was actually working as an accountant for a mental hospital. Without feeling the need to explain herself, she put an end to my current crusade. She stepped in and made me explain myself, listened carefully, and then told me how it was going to be. My grandfather was the only one who thought that the current music was sinful and did not object to my behavior.

They all had, however, become weary of my proselytizing. I needed them to understand they were going straight to hell, and they just rolled their eyes. I decided to enlist the help of those wiser than me, which was everyone, to get my point across.

Every day after school, I would have valuable input as to the television programming going on in our home. Mind you, there were only three channels. Back then there was also a committee of people who worked for the industry, surveying the morality of the programming. I, however, was going to be the judge of that.

I remember a controversial commercial that was all the buzz because it mentioned the word "diarrhea." In reality, our television viewing was tame and left me not much in the way of moral wiggle room. *The Flintstones* and *Gilligan's Island* were not even very good television, let alone depraved. The worst thing you could say was that Ginger dressed provocatively and the Howells were alcoholics.

I was a voracious reader and was confident that our books were the classics and did not require going over. The magazines and comic books, however, were another matter. Especially ones like *Teen Beat* that had celebrities on the cover luring you into a sinful lifestyle. I threw away all my copies, shedding a tear for the ones with the Jackson 5 and the Osmonds on the cover. My brothers threatened me within an inch of my life if I tried to touch their comics that featured the well-endowed female superheroes.

My brothers' protestations brought my mother to her breaking point, and it was time for her to intercede on their behalf. She expressed that I had the right to make my own moral decisions, but I was not to guilt or impose my will on anyone else. These decisions were between each individual and God. Even if I felt they were wrong.

I had never seen Bethany's dad overly emotive. He was kind and pleasant and always positive, but just a calm, intentional man. He could not stop laughing at my naïveté. He was so gracious to explain to me that while the spirit of my desire to alter my lifestyle to be more in keeping with my relationship with Jesus was genuine, the legalistic manner in which I went about it was coming up short. I was also not assigned the gift of judgement and for that matter, no one was. Very well.

My youth pastor was equally merciful. He showed me where in the Word of God I was to take instruction and make my walk with the Lord obedient. Even though I should take a good look at what I was allowing to speak into my life, I was to allow the Lord to instruct and discipline me personally and not to accost my family and friends into the same conclusions. That my new lifestyle would speak for itself and possibly Jesus. I believe my brothers went to him in gratitude for stopping my tirade.

I came to realize that a life that represents my faith and values would do more to show others Jesus than any words ever could. That having a strong foundation would allow me to enjoy music or a school dance and not have it throwing me into a tailspin of sin. So many things can be used to draw us into immoral activity; it is up to us to choose our level of in-dulgence.

My Jesus graciously showed me that I could do nothing to lose or lessen His love for me and that I needed to show that to the rest of the world.

Chapter 12

Handle the Truth

"Go forward bravely. Fear nothing."

–Joan of Arc

I stood down from my Joan of Arc stance and realized once again I was alone in this. This is how it is supposed to be. My relationship with my King was just beginning, and just as with a child learning something new, I had to start at the beginning. Most of the knowledge I had gathered up to this point about the church, God, Jesus, and how I was to conduct myself in the world had some reorganizing to do.

The Christian Bible church I was currently attending held the Bible as truth and represented what a genuine relationship with Jesus looks like. I had only been exposed to religions that directed that relationship through humans where it acquired extra trappings not intended for that relationship.

I had my Bible and my King. While I could sit under the teachings of my pastor, and that is a good thing, we are supposed to have an intimate relationship with Jesus.

There were no resources that I was aware of at that time. Definitely not Google searches or the internet. I did not know that you could purchase commentaries or Bible study guides and wasn't even aware they existed. I assumed because of my experiences with the Catholic church that the pastor was the one to break it down for me.

Actually, I may have sort of invented the original internet search, by using my grandparents' Encyclopedia Brittanica. The original Wikipedia, only with actual facts. The set of encyclopedias were alphabetized, and like a lot of school curriculum, they contained actual historical and biblical facts.

I would sit down with the volume that contained the specific subject matter I was on and gather loads of information. They were written by scholars and educational institutions and the people who actually lived the history and therefore had great information in regard to history and context.

The Bible I had was a King James version, and I loved how it read. A lot of people find it hard to understand the scriptures that way, but I find myself quoting a scripture with my pastor in the King James translation while he is quoting something a tad more readable.

My grandparents also had this really cool book of languages. It was from the 1600s, and it contained about thirty languages in kind of a dictionary format. Greek and Hebrew were two of the languages in this dictionary, as well as being two of the original languages in which the Bible was written.

This made understanding the guidance and instruction being given to me in the Word of God that much more insightful.

* * *

My first inclination to read the entire Bible in a year came at this time. An article in the Christian publication *Our Daily Bread* had spurred the suggestion. I was a voracious reader, and so the daunting task of reading the Bible through in a year's time came as sort of a challenge for me. Not in the way I believe my King hoped.

I wanted to be in the *Guinness Book of Records* for the record time in reading it. As of this writing, the record is seventy-six hours. Mind you, I had no idea of any record; I was just arbitrarily going to claim the crown. For the record, I took six months the first time I read it through.

Having a photographic memory helped me retain more than one would think for the mad rush I had been in to read the Bible through. It was not, however, the point that the Bible reading plan had in mind. Nor that of the Author of this beautiful love letter. I had missed the point, and upon my proclamation to my youth pastor, I became aware of the true benefits and purpose of taking the full year to complete the task.

To quote *Star Trek*'s Khan, "Shall we begin?" With a new sense of purpose and having gathered some wisdom from those who had gone before, I started a genuine reading and study of the Bible in a year. I had been given a Bible by my church family the night I got saved, and it was the prized possession I was going to utilize in this endeavor.

I had a small quandary though. Was I going to be struck by lightning for putting markings in it? Would I drop dead like those who had touched the Ark of the Covenant? Almighty God is pretty serious about the handling of His Word. After receiving reassurance that marking and note-taking in the margins was an acceptable practice, a beautiful piece of my spiritual journey commenced.

* * *

I was armed with my language dictionary that helped me understand when the King James pronunciation required interpretation. The Greek meaning of so many things in the Bible really bring depth to the understanding of what Yahweh truly wanted us to hear.

I had timeline charts and maps that showed how things were in biblical times so I could have context. My further drill-down began to slow my roll in regard to keeping within the 365 days. I was, however, enjoying myself so thoroughly that I decided not to care.

I wanted to be a history teacher when I was in school, and every bit of my studying was like catnip. It all even spilled over into my classwork and gave me great glee to provide a tidbit that even my teachers had not discovered. While the Bible is not a history book, it gave incredible insights into rock-solid historical things.

Prayer was not comfortable for me at the start. Even by myself. It did not occur to me to pray before, during, or after my Bible reading. The only time I had ever been present for prayer was led by others. Not kids. This did not prevent my heavenly Father from getting His point across as I plodded along. By the time I got to Psalms and Proverbs, the thought process was sinking in, and it was made more abundantly clear in the gospels.

Reading the Bible cover-to-cover may not always be the best plan for a new believer. It was, however, His best plan for me. I was born asking "Why?" and on many occasions my mother shoved a book at me to stop my relentless pursuit of knowledge by quizzing her to death. Perhaps the Holy Spirit was her guiding light for that little trick.

Listening to radio and television preachers, along with the sermons at church, all helped to provide context and some interpretation to what I had read as well. The best part of it was that without knowing it, I laid the foundation for my relationship with my King to be about just me and Him. Rock-solid truth right from the start.

He had been teaching me to hear his voice from the first wound. His balm for my little soul was understanding.

* * *

Throughout this year, I learned more about how living out my faith should look as well. By honoring my mother and how she felt about all of this, she began to soften to not only allow me to attend church weekly, but also to attend activities and serve as well.

I drove everyone at church crazy asking if I could help. Preparing the Lord's Supper cups and crackers, cleaning any and every room in the building. Preparing food for events and the little kids' Sunday School. I wanted to be helpful, and more importantly, needed.

My youth pastor's wife came to the rescue. She coordinated the opportunity for me to be a part of the teen prayer group as well as serve in the kitchen when there was any kind of food-related event. Prayer group terrified me, but the kitchen was my wheelhouse. My first real taste of the blessing of serving others was actually the blessing that showed me how I had been serving my family my whole life.

Most of my friends who attended my church were in band or chorus at school, and therefore making music was their "serving" at church. Obviously, the big productions were Easter and Christmas at churches around the globe. Once they heard my singing, they asked me to do a speaking part in the Christmas pageant instead.

Speaking to people right in front of me was terrifying enough. Now they wanted me to be up on a stage? My part was the angel who appeared to the shepherds. Most churches back then had a platform. You could not call it a stage because this was where the Word of God was delivered and not a performance, for heaven's sake. There would be a choir loft that rose up behind the platform. Our church had an opening in the wall behind the choir where a gigantic cross was on the inset wall, and the baptismal was back there, too.

Clearly, as the angel announcing Christ's birth, my part would be at the end of the production. The geniuses in charge decided to put plywood over the baptismal and have me walk out onto it and make my proclamation. I was dressed in a white tablecloth with a hole cut in it and a golden pipe cleaner halo, as tradition would have it.

The house lights went down. The music became dramatic. I was to step out, wave my arm upward and begin, "Fear not . . ." Upon the upward swing of my arm and the pronunciation of the "not," I went crashing into the baptismal waters. The plywood did not exactly fit across its width. And I was, shall we say, sturdy. There was no dove that flew away, and I did not hear a booming voice saying anyone was well pleased.

I scrambled up looking like a drowned cat and finished my lines to the roar of the congregation. It felt like a skit from *The Carol Burnett Show*. I was mortified and a big hit all at the same time. I know of at least a few hundred people who will never forget those "tidings of great joy." I remember the entire speech to this day. This was merely the beginning of my embarrassment in the name of service.

* * *

The winter that ensued after that particularly eventful holiday season was historic in its devastation. Us kids loved it because there were almost four weeks of snow days. Although cabin fever did begin to set in, and my mother was already done with the weather. Her job had her driving seventy-two miles round-trip, and this was the last straw.

My grandparents could not take more winters like this, either. Even though this was the home my grandfather had built for himself and my grandmother to retire to, they were the ones to instigate the move. My mother did not require cajoling to get on board.

In January, the halfway point of my sophomore year, we sat down as a family and were given the news. Moving was not unusual for us. But this was more. They may as well have told me we were moving to the moon. I was not stupid; I had learned geography in school. I just had never bothered to understand where anywhere but Michigan was as a course of living in reality.

My world had just begun to find its footing. There were no threats to my mental and emotional health. No beatings, yelling, or punishment. I had only been a believer for a short while. Other than normal teenage angst, there was no real drama happening. I was going to have to leave my church. I was leaving my Bethany.

The pain was indescribable. The void was galactic, and no sound was coming out from my heart's cry. I did not understand why I was being taken away from people who were so good for me after a lifetime of those who were evil having access.

There was no debate. We were moving to Arizona. My grandparents were going out ahead of us, around springtime. We were waiting for us kids to get out of school and leave during the summer. Six months. I had six months to untangle my heart and spirit from my Bethany. To say goodbye to my church family and have them pray over me to find a good church home when I got there.

After a short tour around Michigan saying goodbye to family, we left. I was crying looking out the window, and it turned ugly when I saw the sign saying "Welcome to Indiana" marking our departure from Michigan. Was God going to give me someone to replace my Bethany? Did He have a church for me where we were going? And how would I find it?

My heart did not feel like it could heal from this break. This wound would take every bit of strength I had to press into Jesus. He had me this far, there would be no doubt He would carry me through. But there was never a promise that life wouldn't hurt.

Chapter 13

Academically Speaking

"Education is what remains after one has forgotten
what one has learned in school."

–Albert Einstein.

It felt like surgery without anesthetic. Removing my father from
my life. Our lives. He was still my father. And yet the scars on
my brain left me questioning myself even more. I had his lack
of belief in me as fuel. Now, would I be able to still prove him
wrong? Or would I fail as completely as he had predicted?

I was in high school now, and the stakes were higher. There
were people who were as competitive as I was vying to be top
dog. It did not occur to me that at any time in the entire world
there were billions of people who knew more than me. I was in
my bubble, and proving myself there was all I knew.

Schoolwork and reading were simultaneously my fantasy safe space and actual reality. I absorbed everything I read, heard, or lived. My mother said I was born asking, "Why?" I wanted to believe I could learn. I wanted to believe that everything I was learning was real. I wanted to believe there was a whole life out there that was not like mine.

None of the other students around me knew anything about me. Actually, no one at all knew anything about me. I had never been asked what I thought about anything. This, however, was the lens through which I viewed the world. There were times that I would even challenge my teachers just to confirm that what I was learning was real.

I am an introverted extrovert, and speaking in front of a class terrified me. Speaking "in" class on the other hand was another matter. My teachers found themselves in a quandary as to what to do about me. I was at the top of my class academically and was always done with any assignment or test extremely early in class. This created an environment in which I had to entertain myself. My teachers did not have the heart to actually punish me, so I was regularly put at a desk in the hall.

Oddly enough, this created a problem of a different sort. I was a bit of an old soul, and my teachers also liked engaging with me and letting me absorb their vast knowledge. So, upon placement in the hall, I would gather the attention of all the teachers who didn't have a class that hour. I was a smart alec and very inquisitive. Usually the teacher who had placed me in the hall would end up coming out to scold me only to stop short, mouth agape at having found me in the middle of a conversation with another teacher.

This was how my school years went from elementary through high school. I met some of my favorite teachers this way and have extremely fond memories. One teacher in my high school in Decatur, Mr. Wunderlin, was truly a kind, caring, and genuine human and teacher. He always made time for any student, to the point of running late for class himself.

He was typically my partner in crime and kept me from receiving anything worse than a good shushing for our wise-cracking in the hall. It is interesting to me that most of my favorite teachers, and the ones I had the best connection with, were male. I think perhaps due to the fact that they showed me what an honorable man looks like, and in my world that was hard to come by.

* * *

My photographic memory and my desire for accuracy did not help me win friends and influence people. My poor teachers tried to run interference, but they were not appreciative of being corrected, either. Even if I was correct. The fact that my father told me that my grades meant nothing, and I would be nothing without him, gave me a drive with a vengeance to excel mentally and academically.

The measuring stick for achievement was, of course, the quarter-end report card. The bane of my brothers' existence, even though they had good grades. They hated hearing my enthusiasm. My mother and stepfather had made a pact with us that we would receive money based on the alphabet of our grades. I got seven dollars for each A, and there were eight classes per quarter. I did not care how much money the other grades received because it was never a concern.

I do not question the logic of how they arbitrarily came up with seven dollars, I just took it to the bank. I joke that I was suicidal if I got an A-, and while I would never make light of suicide, I was really quite obsessed. On top of the personal victory of the grades themselves, I was putting away the cash, too. Sadly, I did not stop to consider how anyone else felt about my achievement or my vocality.

All of this made me "believe" that my father was wrong, and that I was going to be all right. It did not occur to me in my exhausted little brain that I had a bunch of stuff in there along with the knowledge that affected me and needed to come out.

How we are created, and specifically our brains, truly is a miracle. We can have a renewing of our minds. Forgetting what has happened to us will never happen. Understanding and growing from it and allowing our mind to utilize that memory going forward is how Jesus showed me that there, in fact, is healing that begins at the very moment of the wound.

Chapter 14

Mind Games

"If I only had a brain."

–The Scarecrow in The Wizard of Oz

My relentless pursuit of knowledge left me remembering every-thing and utilizing nothing. I engaged in other areas of life, but not with the fervor I pursued my academics. This meant that my skills in other areas left little to be desired. And on top of that, I did not even notice until something awkward or embar-rassing happened.

Life is tricky. It is rarely logical because it is made up of humans. In my world, humans that were teenagers had even less common sense to go on. I was so concerned with the con-sumption of information and its application in an academic setting that I did not develop the application in other areas of my life.

Every muscle, if we use it, has memory and growth, or it atrophies. My mind had been working overtime since the beginning of my abuse that I did not consciously stop to access anything else.

Oddly enough, no one around me seemed to think anything was wrong with me. No one noticed that I only had a few friends and no boyfriends. Not even a sign of interest. I couldn't drive yet, and we lived in a rural area, so I had no neighborhood kids to hang out with. We lived in a single-wide trailer, and yet I did not really even interact much with my brothers.

My stepfather became a long-haul truck driver and was on the road a lot at this time. My mother had a long drive to work and back, and basically ate and crashed upon arriving back home. I was having some of the adult duties put back on my plate, and that went even further to make me feel isolated in a world that was not familiar to my friends.

I was helping with the grocery shopping and meal preparation. Laundry was my responsibility as well. Dishes, cleaning the house and some interesting outdoor chores were split with my brothers. I would prep lunches for everyone, including my mother.

Somehow, the responsibility of getting everyone up on time was mine as well. My mother got up the earliest, and during volleyball season she would give me a ride to the school at 5:30 a.m. for practice. Outside of any sports season, I would get her up and packed up with lunch from the previous night's leftovers, and she would drive to work. I was tasked with determining the shower schedule for all of us, since a water heater on a single-wide was limited. So sometimes people who were not morning people had to become so.

Waking up my brothers was a nasty chore indeed. They would argue and yell at me. One of them kicked out at me and caught me right in the stomach. I pled my case with my mother to make them take care of themselves. My mother was a tiny woman, but she put the fear of God in us, and when she threatened something, she followed through. So, she wrangled the three of us into the living room and set the record straight. We were all in charge of not only getting ourselves up but preparing our own lunches and figuring out our own shower schedule.

Part of the getting-up-on-time scenario involved the fact that we had to catch the bus or not make it to school that day. The school, and more importantly my mother, had very strict repercussions for missing school.

I believe my brothers thought my mother was joking. Although in regard to parenting, that was not her style. The very next day they did not get up on time. I went about my morning. I did not tiptoe around or make a lot of noise either. Just did what I always did to prepare for school.

We lived along a rural highway, and we were kind of the end of the line. The bus would stop on our side of the road to get us, keep going down to a street just past us that had three farms on it and pick up those kids, then come back down the highway to stop for a family across the highway from us. They did not allow kids to cross this busy street for the bus, so the bus made a stop for them on the way back.

So, I headed out to the side of the road to catch the bus. My brothers were awakened by the door closing as I left. I heard yelling and running. They did not, however, make it out to catch the bus on time. The bus driver was a wonderful lady and she asked where they were. I kept the story to a synopsis, which put her in hysterics. After picking the kids up down the road and as we were on our way to pass our house, the entire busload was bent over laughing watching my brothers run across the field and the highway. The bus driver went a little past the stop before braking, for effect. After that day, I was definitively not the alarm clock for my brothers anymore.

* * *

I loved school. I loved everything about it. I loved learning. I loved the environment. I loved the structure and schedule. I even loved tests. One of my favorite classes, which frankly contained more practical knowledge than all the rest, was Home Economics. I brought real-world experience to the table.

Sewing was not my cup of tea, but getting a bad grade was not an option. I made two perfect blouses for my mother out of wild psychedelic patterns that she thanked me for, and yet I never saw her wearing them. Perhaps she got the irony of the situation, given the outfits she had sewn for us.

Cooking, baking, grocery shopping, and meal preparation were in my blood. My mother and grandmother were two of the best cooks I have ever known. My grandmother even taught me how to can food for the winter. My first badge in Girl Scouts was for cooking. The school was full of farm kids who definitely had chores that would involve meals. I, however, was thrust into the role of chef at eleven years old and could have had my culinary degree at that point in high school.

Our final exam for the fall semester was a Thanksgiving meal. I was in charge of the turkey and made a couple of pies as well. I seriously did not take Home Economics because I believed it to be an easy A grade. And, in fact, several of my honor roll competitors found that out the hard way. I loved it.

It taught practical skills that would be more useful than algebra to me.

* * *

No one took a look at my brain. No one. Ever. With the exception of a Mensa test that said I was a genius, only the school system tested what had been put in there. In fact, when anything about my childhood came out, they looked horrified and pitifully at me and changed the subject. If the adults around me did not know how to help me heal the scars left there, who would?

All of this book learnin' and I had not synced it up with what my brain had been doing to protect me all this time. It was as if they were two different compartments in my brain. The logic and facts of history, math, and science proved themselves out. What had happened to me thus far in my short life was not logical and made no sense.

I had been shown that it was not about me. That I had done nothing wrong. Our minds are given the ability to reason from birth, and every single experience establishes critical thinking. I was given the ability to sort out and detect when my circumstances were heading in a direction that I needed to remove myself.

All of this was training and building muscle memory that would further my healing. It all prepared me to listen to the voice of God as guidance and a warning where necessary. It did not stop me from making bad choices of my own, but it was not for lack of intuition and understanding that it was a path I should not have chosen in the first place.

* * *

The winter having crushed everyone's spirit, the adults had

another confab, and we were on the move. In six months, after my drivers ed class was concluded, we were moving to Arizona in July of 1978. I was not a stupid kid, and I knew that there was more to the world than Michigan. In my mind I had just gotten the pieces on the chessboard where I wanted them. Now, we were going to be playing checkers instead.

We loaded up one big moving van and sent everything to Arizona, where my grandparents would receive it. We moved into a two-bedroom cabin on the campground at Lake of the Woods, closer to town, for our remaining months. I had the remainder of my sophomore year and a softball season to complete, all while sharing a room with my teenage brothers. Nothing awkward to see here.

Those remaining months felt like they were in slow motion. Each individual day felt more like forty-eight hours. And yet, in a blink of an eye and without much fanfare, it was time to move.

We piled into our RV and Suburban and were on our way. I wanted to take in everything on the way out of town and yet could not see clearly through my tears. In a matter of miles, I would be surrounded by nothing I knew.

Body Type

"I'm not overweight. I'm under-tall"

–Garfield

He was as wide as he was tall, with a cigarette was dangling from his mouth. He was outside of the medical clinic as we entered the building. It was midsummer and volleyball tryouts were coming soon. It was time for my sports physical, and my mother had taken time off work to take me.

What exactly were they looking for to confirm my fitness to play a sport? They put me through a bizarre combination of procedures, none of which appeared to have anything to do with any sport I had ever played or any skillset required to play them. And yet, I needed the doctor's sign-off or I couldn't play.

As I understand it, he was a pediatrician. He did not have

a specialty in any particular area other than that. But he listened to my heart, looked up my nose and into my ears. He hit my knees and elbows with a little hammer. He didn't have me swing a bat, run, or set a volleyball. His nurse checked some stuff with a thermometer and a thing that wrapped around my arm, and she pumped it up. They weighed me and checked my height. I had to pee in a cup, which was humiliating. And we had had an outhouse at one point, so that is saying something.

After being left to sit, in a weird gown that opened in the back, for an inordinate amount of time, the doctor finally came back. He looked grim. He spoke to my mother instead of me, which I thought was odd as well. He informed her that he was going to pass me in spite of my being overweight. He made it sound like I was on the precipice of death. He handed her some paperwork and told her we were to go down the hall to the dietician to get my orders for how I was to eat.

The doctor was the man I'd seen outside the building. While I had learned my lesson about smarting off when my father backhanded me ass over teacart in the restaurant, it popped out before I could catch it. Frankly, I didn't imagine the doctor would strike me either. I opened my mouth, and it came out. "YOU, YOU are telling me I'm overweight? YOU are putting me on a diet?"

My mother turned ashen and grabbed my arm. "Shelly, stop it."

You would have thought that was enough of a jolt to stop me, but I was on a roll. "But, Mom, look at him. He has to be over 300 pounds. He was smoking outside, too. What right does he have to tell me I need to lose weight?"

She pulled me in close and whispered, "Do you want to play sports or not? You need his permission, now shut up." She was not wrong and brought me back to reality. I apologized for my outburst, accepted the papers, and we were on our way. The dietician was kind and indicated that I was being put on the National Heart Disease Diet. Oh, goody.

I was not unintelligent, and it had not gotten past me that I had extra sand in my hourglass. My brothers reminded me when it required some form of teasing to win a fight. My loving mother said I was not fat; I was big-boned. Not sure that sounded better, but it gave her a peace about the situation. She also determined that my weight was not that bad and did not make me follow the diet to the letter.

Not even one of the doctors I went to for annual and sports physicals was ever told about what I had been through as a child. I cannot even imagine my response if any of them had heard and decided to look for the wounds. Having to get naked and have them touch me at all brought enough trepidation as it was. Realizing that the very humans that should have been tasked with helping me heal had enough scar tissue of their own makes the fact that my Jesus gave me a deep understanding of my own body that much more precious.

* * *

Tryouts were in a couple of weeks, and I had only played volleyball in gym class at school. I loved it and was determined to at least give it a try. After all I had learned from my childhood best friend Don and his brothers, I was kind of a "jack of all trades, and a master of none" when it came to sports. It allowed me to be good enough to have fun. High school was another matter; they expected talent. They expected wins.

Girls tend to get closer to their full height in high school, while boys fill out afterwards. I was 5'7" and considered a little above average in height for a freshman. I was not going to make the basketball team and didn't like it anyway, but volleyball looked fun and up my alley.

The coach was strict and began whipping us into shape, even at tryouts. There was an incredible series of drills and calisthenics we had to get through before we could even set foot on the court. I would discover later that this would be the procedure every day before I could enter the practice games and drills.

I was not quick and had literally no vertical. I had not needed jumping to this point in my short life. I was the new girl. I was not an athletic specimen. But I did all that was asked of me in the time allotted, and I took to a special setter drill like a fish to water.

The coach wanted setters to do several special drills, but the one that separated the women from the girls was setting a regulation basketball to varying heights for sets of twenty. Jammed and dislocated fingers were aplenty in the setter camp. I excelled at this, and it gave me enough of an edge to make the team. Their best setter had graduated last season, and no one had stepped up.

Because it was a small school and volleyball and basketball season coincided, the girls volleyball team had to practice before school at 5:30 a.m. As an early riser and someone who got all their homework done well in advance, I was thrilled with the situation. My ride, my mother, was not. She did, however, comply and just utilized it as a great way to beat the traffic on her thirty-six-mile drive to work.

I was not what you would consider a handsome girl, and my fashion sense left little to be desired. Volleyball practice kept my slow-motion metabolism relatively in check, and therefore I maintained a mildly average, girly appearance. All of which allowed me to stay hiding behind my walls with good reason for no interest from suitors.

Any time I was in a sport for that season, I felt like I had somewhere safe that I belonged. It did not mean that I wouldn't make mistakes or that we didn't lose games. It was just some-where that if those things did happen, I was not rejected or made to feel ashamed. My coach and I really connected. She knew about a few things, not the abuse, but about the divorce and visitation with my dad, etc . . . She gave me a lot of grace after the weekends we would come back, when I might be off-kilter.

Chapter 16

Birds & Bees

"Nearly everybody gets twitterpated in the springtime."

–*Friend Owl in Bambi*

It was not that I didn't think boys were interesting. It was just that after all I had been through, I didn't quite see a point to them yet. Bethany and Paul tried their best to keep putting Steve and me in chaperone situations with them. We were just not each other's cup of tea. My interaction with him felt more like a brother. We did actually have fun with Bethany and Paul, just not what they had intended. Because of my large bosom, I did attract the wrong kind of attention from some young men, and that put me in a fight-or-flight mode every single time.

There were a couple of guys that made me feel comfortable

enough that I could talk and joke around coming and going to classes. They were probably as terrified as me, and it stayed on an even keel for a while. One young man, Danny, got the courage up to send me the ever popular "Yes" or "No" note asking me to check whether or not I liked him. He was okay, but a tad pushy and overzealous, and that made me uncomfortable. I explained to him that I preferred we stay friends. He did not take it well. He started making me the target of very public teasing.

Our study hall substitute teacher was a really young, pretty lady who could not have been out of her twenties. Needless to say, all the boys were acting up. My jilted suitor was exceptionally so. He would sit on her desk and flirt with her and then come over to me and push my books off the table and ask if I could see that she liked him. I asked her multiple times to make him stop. This only fed his desire to act up and win me over. I, however, snapped.

Having come from a violent childhood, I would never have liked to hit or hurt someone. That being said, Danny went a bridge too far. He came over and started pushing my books off one at a time. I turned to look at the teacher who was laughing, along with pretty much everyone else.

Next came his biggest mistake. He got physical. He put his finger in my face . . . and then poked me in the chest. I do not recall my thought process. I grabbed him by the collar and dragged him down the long table I was sitting at until he fell off the end.

You could hear a pin drop. And then as if I were really saved by the bell, the dismissal bell went off. It took me a minute to collect my things, and I was the last to leave, avoiding eye contact with the teacher as I went.

As I exited the class into the hall, my older brother was

 118

passing and said something to the effect of, "Right on, Sis, don't let anyone push you around." Other kids were high-fiving me and making similar statements. Needless to say, any hopes of dating were dashed. It was now known in all the land that you were not to trifle with Michele Vrabel.

* * *

Considering I had now struck fear into even the slightest possibility of a boyfriend or date, I decided to look at being Bethany's chaperone as a social experiment that I hoped would teach me dating etiquette and social graces. The fact that Steve and I teased each other more than my brothers and I did was not going to deter me from trying to learn something.

Their next date was a bit of a road trip to an ice cream shop in the next town over. Ice cream seemed safe and sounded like fun. Like the secret service acting as an advance team and surveying the surroundings for risk assessment, I concluded that there was nothing that Bethany could utilize for any dramatic effect in keeping Paul's attention. Which was hilarious in the first place because he was totally twitterpated.

There were only a couple of families besides our little group in the ice cream shop. We got our banana splits and glasses of water and made our way to a corner table. We were having fun talking about school being out for the summer soon. This made Bethany and me sad, since I would be moving away, and Paul and Steve weren't familiar with all the details because they were not in my brothers' friend groups and had not been caught up on the gossip.

The conversation about missing all of them and the adventures we had been through led to a bit of heated debate as to whether they were fun for everyone or not. Steve was also coming to the realization that he would now have to handle chaperone duties on his own. I was not looking so bad now, was I?

Bethany feigned offense and lobbed a spoonful of whipped cream in the boys' direction. I am not sure if she purposefully missed Paul or was just a bad aim, but she struck a bullseye on Steve. Against Paul's protestations, Steve led the assault. It was like an ice cream version of the game Battleship. At first, I was left out, since Paul was too nice and Steve and Bethany had each other in their sights.

She decided I was laughing too hard, and she also didn't want to be the only one covered in melted ice cream. This was an ugly turn of events, for even our sweet Paul nailed me right between the eyes. Thankfully, my glasses were still on and gave me a modicum of protection. We cleaned up as best we could, but I believe that Paul's family car was sticky for a while after this particular date.

* * *

The anxiety about our move and our weird living conditions in a temporary cabin space had my body really struggling. The drills and routines of the remaining softball season kept my health in check and at the very least aided in my sleep. I would crash by the time I got home at night and sometimes barely eat. I was fasting before it was cool. Belonging to a team felt good. Being good at what I was asked to do for them felt awesome.

My last softball season in Decatur was incredible. We were really coming together as a team and starting to draw a crowd, even with baseball and track having competing schedules. My mom was able to make it to more games this season because she was leaving her job for our move. Her workload had been diminished, and she got off work in time to be in the stands.

The excitement and camaraderie kept my mind off our departure, if only for those innings.

Driver's education was part of the public school system when I was in high school and therefore was mandatory at no cost to the parents. It was always conducted over the summer and usually taught by teachers who wanted the work year-round.

There was another teen who started off with me as soon as school ended. Toward the end of June when we were getting into rural and highway driving, for some reason, I was on my own with the teacher.

He was a nice man and very patient. I cannot say that being alone with a grown man did not make me nervous. He was nice-looking, and the fact that I very consciously took note of this was putting me a tad on edge. He did nothing to make me feel anything other than safe and like we were in this car to teach me how to drive it.

While going through my rural driving paces, he started giving me directions to his home, since he needed to go there for something. He had absolutely no clue about me or my life. I was a student driver, period. His sudden need to go to his house set off terrors in me that he couldn't have known about.

Every terrifying scenario was coursing through my mind and body. The thought of how I would get out of the car and when we would be practically in the middle of nowhere. It took all I had not to start crying. I was gripping the steering wheel so hard; it was the only reason I was not visibly shaking.

As I pulled into his driveway, there was a woman on the porch—his wife. He was going by to pick up the lunch she had prepared for him. I was a student. A ridiculous little teenager, and he had no need to explain himself. In any other universe this would have been just a destination on a driving course.

I passed the course, and this poor man had no idea how much I had truly been tested.

* * *

With each and every move of our family, I felt the breach in the walls that had finally come down rise again. While I cannot say that I had any enthusiasm about this new adventure, I was genuinely comforted that He had me. He was not going to leave His daughter to flounder. My Comforter had a plan.

This was goodbye. No more sleepovers. No more divinity. No more Bethany. I did not dwell in the lament of this goodbye. It would never occur to me to defy my mother and stay anyway. Not that Bethany's dad would have allowed it either. My safe space was being left behind in Michigan.

Season III

INTO THE DESERT

Chapter 17

Whole New World

"When you can't make them see the light,
make them feel the heat."

–Ronald Reagan

Lewis and Clark would have benefitted from my mother's mapping skills. She used an old school paper atlas to map out our journey to Arizona. Adventures were planned in every state to relieve the tedium of the long stretches of driving.

She loved making charcoal imprints of historical markers and graves, so she sprinkled in a fair amount of those. There were a couple of amusement parks, national parks, and bizarre truck stops as a nod to our stepfather. We stayed in our RV at many unique places, including some KOA campgrounds. These allowed for a real full-size shower that didn't give me claustrophobia, as well as bathrooms that did not telegraph what the previous occupant's business happened to be.

We had a good time for the most part and got to see a lot of the country as we went. I settled into the idea that there was no going back and that I needed to find the good in what was about to happen to me. The geography as we went along was extremely different from Michigan's, as were the temperature and level of humidity. When we got to my grandparents' home in Arizona in July, the temperature was over 120 degrees. Seriously, Dante's Inferno come to life.

My grandparents had acquired a house already and had found a place for us as well. The heat was oppressive. After living my whole life in Michigan, this type of extreme heat had never occurred to me . . . ever. It felt like you were opening the oven to check on your cookies nonstop. I was not built to walk around naked or in short "Daisy Duke" cut-off shorts. But there was seriously no level of clothing that did not add to the discomfort.

* * *

It was July, and we had a couple of weeks to get into the school system and sign up for sports. My one salvation. I have never been very self-confident. I have, however, felt at home in academics and my preferred sports. I actually have a pretty competitive spirit in these areas. I was anxiety-ridden due to going to a new school and having to head into tryouts for coaches I had never met and with players I did not know. My new high school in Arizona was bigger than the entire school system I had just come from, which meant a deeper pool of talent.

Volleyball tryouts were first up and probably my most comfortable lane. As I entered the gym, everyone was just milling around waiting for tryouts to begin. My coaches in Michigan were strict about a certain set of drills and routines prior to getting into the actual practice of the game.

I was used to running wind sprints, taking on the bleachers

from end to end, sit-ups, wall-sits, and then as a setter, I used to have to set with a basketball through various drills. All of this needed to be completed before I could enter the practice game.

As I stepped out and began my routine, the other players were astonished and snickering. I was not to be dissuaded. They stood around pointing and laughing at my decision to run drills without being instructed to do so. I did not have the build of an athlete at all. However, it had only been a few months since softball season had ended, and my conditioning got me through my drills without collapsing, in spite of the heat.

The coaches entered the gym with mouths agape and then, to the bemusement of the onlooking players, chose to tell all the players to follow my lead. To say I was unpopular at this moment is an understatement. Most of the players were just mad at me and made a lame attempt at copying my moves. Some, who I found out later were the players that had some humility and talent, came to me to ask the drill.

It was still over 110 degrees outside, and the gym ran on only evap coolers. This left a heap of wheezing young ladies looking not too happily in my direction. Then we got down to tryouts. They perked up now, and after some posturing, made it seem like we would now separate the women from the girls.

I was a setter and good defensive player, but my best weapon was my serve. I could place it anywhere I wanted and could toy with the players on the opposing team. The coach had us work on the overall skills of the tryouts first, and then we would break into our individual position tryouts. The head coach had a service drill that involved chairs being placed on the opposite side of the net for us to hit when so instructed as we stepped up to the line. This was a Zen space for me, and I could block out everyone: teammates, opposing fans—peace.

I was not perfect at anything but good enough to be a solid

addition to the team and players with more talent if they were disciplined enough to listen and take advantage of the assists I brought to the table. Once these skills were being performed for the tryout, I started to gather that I was garnering the respect of the other players. They also began to realize that if they were a setter, they might need to up their game. I made the team and felt at least one piece fall into place that lowered my anxiety and gave me emotional stability.

* * *

Academics came with the same challenges. As with any school, there is typically a set of kids firmly ensconced in the upper ranks of class. Truthfully, it was never me against them. It has always been me against me. Am I enough? Can I cut it . . . without my dad? Classes at grade level have been less than challenging for me since the fourth grade. So, off I headed into Advanced Placement classes out of the gate. Go big or go home. During the '70s there were not a lot of advanced classes, since public education was pretty good and usually covered those bases. I did, however, get into Advanced English and Economics classes. I also started attending community college, since my high school schedule ended shortly after lunch.

My Advanced Placement English class was an eclectic group of students. Most of the debate team, and coincidentally the highest-ranking members of the class, were the bulk of the roster. An athlete that had his life all mapped out to get a great college scholarship and then on to pro football was seated next to me. We became fast friends, and he asked for my collaboration when it was allowed. He excelled in all sports, but football was his game. He was incredibly handsome, kind, and sweet. His popularity gave me some social street cred I did not even know possible. It made for a fun year in AP English, and we gave the debate kids a scare.

My social circle settled into a bizarre little group of friends who had an area marked out to meet for lunch each day. Most of us were believers and sometimes at lunchtime would entertain theological conversations. We had kids from all the typical high school groups: jocks, geeks, band members, theater kids, etc . . . Every class was represented as well. This was my junior year and so seniors were not shunning me, and the underclassmen weren't afraid of me, so I felt safe for the time being.

A handful of Christian young ladies from my church and others started to form friendships that included activities and sleepovers outside the bounds of school. It was in this area that a couple of fateful firsts got their opportunity to pounce.

* * *

One of the senior girls, Bea, had several of us out to her house for a sleepover. We were also going to attend a social event at her church that evening. At this social function, there were a lot of high school kids, both male and female, in attendance who did not go to our high school but rather one that was more rural. She fancied a young man, Jeff, a lifeguard, who was several years older than us, but she felt their values did not align and never staked a claim on him.

Jeff was introduced to us at this event, and he took an immediate interest in me. I was incredibly naïve, and he had all the right moves. He told me he thought I was pretty and took an interest in everything I had to say.

Bea announced immediately upon his show of interest that he currently was dating someone at our high school. This caused him to change his approach in my direction by appearing to simply want to get to know one of her friends. He was not initially aggressive in the expression of his interest, since he was in fact seeing someone. I began noticing his car in the parking lot at school when he was picking up a young lady regularly.

A couple of months passed, and Jeff came by Bea's house when I was there and announced he was no longer seeing anyone. This alone did not release me to feel at ease about his advances. He took his time and even asked to come to my house and meet my mom. I was sixteen and he was twenty-one. He was charming and funny and had my mom in the palm of his hand. He did not rush anything and gave the appearance of genuine interest. He had a plan.

My "love language" is words of affirmation, and he had a truckload of them. At some point he even threw in that he loved me. He would come to my house with a buddy, and we would play cards with my mom. Sometimes we played golf and went to the movies. He took me to softball games he played in and introduced me as his girl. I had been to his home to have dinner with his parents.

We went on actual dates, and he slowly introduced touching me: hand-holding, arm around my shoulders, and hugs good-night as he was leaving. I was terrified and thrilled at the same time. When I was a child, this behavior was headed toward horrors of abuse. This was someone close to my age, telling me what someone who likes you should say, with promises of love and connection to assuage fears. He had a plan.

After a couple of months of dating, he introduced further touching. As they used to say, "rounding a couple bases." Soon his car was showing up at school to pick me up. He expressed being a Christian and understanding what that meant to my purity. However, he now "loved" me and that made it all different. That was all I should need to allow us to consummate our relationship. He had a plan.

* * *

Jeff invited me to his house for dinner and a movie. He did not inform me that his folks would not be home. There was, in fact, dinner and a movie. He had a great stereo system in his room and Steely Dan was playing. He took me by the hand and walked me to a couch in his room which folded out into his bed. He did not bother; it stayed a couch.

He made it all about me and stifled my protests by covering my mouth with kisses and holding my arms at my sides. Of course, his words and this type of intimacy made me feel that someone genuinely wanted me also.

It did not matter that neither of us was fully undressed. Just that there was access. It took all of a few minutes and tears were streaming down my face as he finished. It was not pleasant. It did not feel good. I did not feel loved. He ushered me out the door.

This was not his first rodeo, and he knew what he needed to do to pull off the self-gratification he was looking to achieve. He had worked his way into being my first sexual encounter. He had every intention of conducting several more and comforted me into believing he loved me and that this was okay. He had gotten what he wanted and was going to put on a full-court press to get more. He was determined to convince me that he genuinely loved me and that it would "feel better."

I was horrified thinking that everyone would be able to look at me and see what I had done. He was a smooth talker, and I did not break it off, and in fact we continued as a couple for several more months. I was sixteen and not stupid, just emotionally unintelligent. As with each layer of abuse I had encountered in my life, this brought up the walls and I withdrew from everyone. He had a plan.

* * *

We were heading into summer, and the heat was unbearable. I was feeling nauseous and tired for no apparent reason. Jeff picked me up from school early because I called him and told him I was not feeling well. He had a huge smile on his face and acted like he had won some championship. He knew what was wrong and had the solution.

I was pregnant. I almost passed out. I was sixteen. I was not married. I could not process who I was letting down first. What would my mom say? What would my friends who I thought did not even know I was having sex say? What would God say?

Mr. Wonderful interrupted my diatribe of shame going on in my head with his brilliant thoughts on the matter. Not that his bright idea of not wearing a condom or even checking to see if I knew what birth control was had been the best so far. He laughed and remarked that the solution was simple. He would take me to get an abortion and pay for it and everything.

"What is an abortion?"

"I take you to this place called Planned Parenthood and they make it all go away," he said.

This was 1978, and Roe v Wade was pretty new, and I had never heard of it or abortion. The only "sex education" I had had up to this point had been my experiences being molested. I did not understand the workings of birth control either. I do not say any of this to blame someone else for my choices. Just to explain where I was as a frightened teenage girl.

None of this felt right. I could not ask anyone what I should do. It would mean exposing that I had had sex. Every bit of this tore at my fragile soul. I had replaced listening to the voice of Jesus with that of my boyfriend. He knew what to say and how to make it sound like the right thing to do. He had a plan.

* * *

I had been attending the softball games he played in for a local team, and he suddenly asked me not to come to a game. Bea said she was going and asked me to come anyway. As we were sitting in the stands, we both had a surprising introduction. A young lady and her family were visiting from Texas and were there to watch her boyfriend. Coincidentally, the same boyfriend I was cheering on. I did not announce my connection to him but was devastated, and my friend and I left.

Every fiber of my being understood that I had allowed this to happen to me. I had not prayed about entering a relationship with this man. I had not put myself in a position to maintain any kind of purity by having chaperones as I had done for my Bethany. I stopped listening to the one voice that could have helped me protect myself.

He did not reach out or connect in any way for several weeks and then suddenly popped up again. He did not want to go on dates, just wanted to either come to my house, his house, or his car, to have sex. He openly admitted that he was merely dating virgin girls to take care of himself until his marriage and was quite smug about how ingenious he thought he was.

He ended our relationship shortly thereafter. I discovered that his fiancée had graduated college and was now moving to Arizona to marry him. I felt so used and disposable. Once again, someone who was supposed to love me or at least said he did, absolutely did not. I take full responsibility for my own actions. However, I did not look to anyone else to blame for this man's behavior other than himself.

Walls up. Trust down. Communicating with no one. One broken little girl with a side order of vulnerability.

Chapter 18

Rebel With a Cause

> "I am the prodigal son every time I search for
> unconditional love where it cannot be found."
>
> *–Henri Nouwen*

I lived a life that would make the prodigal son look like a Boy Scout. I am not proud of this and do not brag. I am simply stating that while living this way and making these choices, my King was still waiting and watching for me to return. I made choices that were not healthy for any area of my life and would ultimately have a mostly negative impact on my future choices.

The first arena I stepped into was college, where I made the choice to live in the dorms. Wrong answer. Satan saw me coming. The decision to live in the dorms would open old wounds and create many new ones. My Jesus made his voice heard loud enough to keep me from total devastation. I had lost weight, cut my hair, gotten contact lenses, and had a whole new exterior for my senior year in high school. I managed to maintain this look heading into college. I was also now familiar with the pleasures of sex and was in desperate need of attention. I was completely unprepared for what was about to hit me. My first dip into the world of alcohol came at this time as well, and that did not bring sound judgement with it, to say the least.

I had a couple of "encounters" in my first semester but ended that semester with a new boyfriend. I guess in reality I have always been someone who wanted monogamy. He was kind and treated me very well. He was a good ole boy, liked country music, and behaved like a gentleman. He would open doors and pull out chairs for me. We made it through to the summer, but when he went back home, a high school sweetheart stole his heart.

My last year at Central Arizona College was filled with excelling at academics and a healthy smattering of partying. There were, of course, sexual encounters; however, there was no one to blame for these other than myself. My heart had reconciled that since I had already committed this particular sin, what was the harm?

My poor choices were adding up, and I was allowing them to shape my relationships going forward. I decided I did not want to get my heart involved. I was going to enjoy the company of a guy, and if he got too attached . . . it was time to move along.

* * *

I have always liked healthy, fit, athletic men. They seemed to like me, too. I dated various baseball and basketball players, with a few rodeo cowboys thrown in for good measure. The good news for my heart was that none of them seemed too interested in falling in love at this point either, so I did not have to test my "love 'em and leave 'em" philosophy. I was just having fun without much concern for the future.

After my two years of scholarship money ran out, I was out of money to complete my degree. My family did not have the ability to help either. I had worked in Phoenix during the summers of my college years and gotten some contacts for both jobs and places to live, so I packed up my Pinto and moved to Tempe and did not look back.

I had graduated high school at seventeen and therefore was only nineteen when I took on the workplace in Phoenix. I was working for a company in the construction industry, and at that time it was really no place for a little girl. Divine intervention kept me safe in my workplace, and I learned a great deal. My extracurricular activity at happy hours with one of my co-workers was another story altogether.

A dear friend to this day, Denise and her live-in boyfriend adopted me, and I would end up spending all of my after-work hours and weekends enjoying a party, concert, or some type of activity with all of our mutual buddies and anybody else who decided to tag along. I discovered a healthy tolerance for holding my liquor. It was the '80s, and I once again found myself in the company of dates who were not looking to "put a ring on it" anytime soon.

While I loved the party girl lifestyle I had carved out for myself and had not done irreparable harm to my heart yet, I felt the desire for something more adventurous rise up in me. I decided I wanted to spread my wings and move to California. I had met some people at a college business executive competition and heard through the grapevine that one of the guys, Alan, was looking for a roommate in the Los Angeles area.

This did not go over well with my mother because of the reputation that Los Angeles had garnered for all types of crime.

I found a headhunter agency, and they got me a job that paid extremely well, and the move was on. My mother began laying out magazine articles on the crime statistics in California in hopes that I would be deterred. I probably should have been, but everything was working out and my new roommate was a guy, so I figured I had at least some security.

I spent two years living in Van Nuys, California, and learned a great deal working for a Big 8 accounting firm. Originally, I was in the tax department and helped one of the partners there write a tax manual for the government. The audit department was my next excursion, and I learned a lot about forensic accounting there.

I continued my decision to be in control of who "loved" me and who I wanted to move along. The idea of control is laughable. I caused more pain to myself with this strategy, since I did not have a steady guy, and it rang hollow. Partying had its fun, but waking up alone or not really having someone to share good news or day trips with exposed a void.

While I grew my skill sets and had the beginnings of a great résumé, even for a twenty-one-year-old, I did not, however, cultivate great character or add to the maturity of my soul. I went out a lot. I dated a lot. No genuine connections were made or even concerned me.

During my entire time in California the first time, I cannot honestly say that any person or experience made a lasting impact on my life. There were lots of really cool people, and it was not for lack of their relationship to me. The walls I had up to keep people from claiming to love me and then reject me were just too high.

137

* * *

While living in California in the early '80s, I went on vacation to Hawaii at Christmas and again six months later. It was so amazing that I decided to do a little research and determine if I would like to make another move.

I brought a local paper home with me from the second trip and found some employment agencies to reach out to and see what the job market was like. On the first trip, I had met a couple who owned a local tour company and had used their services the second time as well. I figured they would be a great resource once I got back to the islands.

I packed up and flew there with a one-way ticket and a week's hotel reservation. My brother was in the Navy, and his ship had been stationed in Hawaii from San Diego one month before I went. It was great to have someone there I knew, and he even picked me up at the airport.

One of the employment agencies I had reached out to had several opportunities for me, and I was hired on my first day of interviews. I stopped by the tour agency just to say hello and perhaps put some feelers out for a place to live, and a young lady they had working for them was in fact leaving her living situation, and they needed a new roommate. I managed to find a job and a place to stay with roommates within two days and then partied the remainder of the week until I started work.

My apartment was in the heart of Waikiki. It was a short bus ride to my workplace and extremely convenient for going out on the weekends. I had two roommates, Karen and Vickie. Vickie and I are still friends to this day. We hit it off right away, and our work and play schedules matched up perfectly.

Every weekend, we would go out on Friday and Saturday nights, and we would spend all day on Saturday and Sunday at the beach. Our tastes in nightclubs and the men who congregated there were similar and made making plans a breeze. It was a great situation, and I was beginning to feel like my heart and soul were finding a safe space.

* * *

I did not see him coming. I had every intention of utilizing the same relationship approach that had been supposedly keeping me safe. That lasted about a month. He was tall, dark, and handsome. A Marine named Bill who looked like a real-life GI Joe. He picked me. That was all it took. He was kind, loving, and attentive. He liked being nearby and having a hand on me. That had driven me mad in the past. He was dreamy, and nothing he did annoyed me.

He had to leave for maneuvers on the Big Island two weeks after we met. We had spent every day together prior to that. He and a buddy snuck to a pay phone so he could call me and sing, "I just called to say I love you." They could not sing a lick, but he had me at hello.

Sirens were going off in my head. Every single human who had said I love you to me thus far used it to lie to and manipulate me. How could someone who had only known me two weeks genuinely love me? I was not listening to my Holy Spirit-given intuition. My heart's guardian was being ignored.

We had three more weeks together when he got word that they were being deployed to Okinawa for six months. I was heartbroken. We spent every day together until he had to leave.

A parting deal he wished to strike was not leaving me feeling hopeful about his return. He thought we should "stay together," but that we could see whomever we wanted and do anything we wanted while he was on deployment.

This did not sound like a good deal to me. I had heard from my brother who had been on deployments what "doing anything we want" meant. We were, however, in the barracks parking lot and they were boarding buses, so I did not want his parting memory to be me being jealous or needy. I kissed him and said goodbye and then went into Waikiki with my roommate and ugly-cried and got ugly-drunk.

* * *

I did go on a few dates during the deployment but wanted to keep my word that we were together and therefore did not get too involved. The six months actually flew by, and when the fleet came back in, well, it was quite a party. Bill and I were together again, and it was incredible . . . for two weeks.

He informed me that someone he had been dating back home was coming to Hawaii for a visit that had been planned for a while. Funny he had not mentioned it before. The shoe finally dropped. The sirens were back.

They would be staying together in base housing, and he would not be able to see me while she was there. He swore that she did not mean more than me and he would miss me the whole time. Um, this sounded familiar.

Bill ended up coming to see me a couple of evenings after all. I still did not feel good about this because I did not want to be a cheater. He assured me that they were not in a "relationship" and after she left, we were back to normal. He told me he loved me and there was talk of more than Hawaii.

During the week, Bill started staying on base more, and we were only together on the weekends. Because of my work schedule, I did not let this bother me. Soon after this, he started going to the beach with his buddies most of the weekend and just coming to see me on Sunday nights on his way back to base. One of his buddies had started dating my roommate, and he had decided to stay with her one of the beach weekends instead of with the guys. He let it slip that my guy had actually started seeing someone else and was camping at this particular beach every weekend with her.

I was devastated. Oddly enough, I thought about his girl back home and how she was probably his forever plan and that I did not want to be that girl, so I ended it and survived better than I would have expected. Bill left me alone, even though there were parties at the beach and the clubs where we would be with our group of friends.

All the Marines in his company considered me "Bill's girl." So, dating another Marine did not seem likely, and I hadn't really thought about it. One young man found the courage and asked to come by my place to talk to me. He was incredibly sweet, handsome, and had the bluest eyes with dark hair . . . my kryptonite. We started dating, and this made Bill decide to try and come back and stake a claim.

He came to a party that he had not been invited to and asked if I could come outside to talk. It was awkward and un-comfortable, but he was not going to leave. He played on my heartstrings and tried to claim that this new girl did not mean anything. I guess that was supposed to make me feel better that someone threw me away for someone else who did not mean anything to him.

However, he was still with her, wanted to stay with her for a bit, and then come back to me. How could I resist an offer such as this? I was someone he could see being with long-term and he wanted to finish sowing his oats because he was two years younger than me.

I told him that if he could find someone who would agree to that type of arrangement, he should hang onto them like grim death. I walked back into the party and only saw him at a celebration party shortly after that for the last time before I left the island.

Even after how Bill had treated me, the other Marines in the company did not like anyone else dating me and decided to give my new guy a hard time. They made his life hard and our time together so awkward that we finally mutually ended it.

My heart decided it had enough at this point, and I was not going to have a "boyfriend" for the foreseeable future. I struck up a friendship with a gigantic Marine officer who looked like a superhero. He was 6'4" tall, with blond hair, blue eyes, and an enormously proportionate bodybuilder's physique. He rode a Harley and worked as a bouncer at one of our favorite night-clubs. He was divorced and had been badly burned by his ex, so we were a perfect fit for not getting crazy.

***

I was home, sick, and lying on the couch watching the space shuttle Challenger launch when it happened. The day the shuttle blew up in 1986 was the same day my grandmother died. This was extremely difficult for my mother, since my grandmother had had stomach cancer, and my mom kept her at home and the amount of caregiving she required as well as the weight on my mother's heart took its toll.

My roommate got married the following month, and, of course, moved out. Her brother, our other roommate, had decided to move back to the mainland. Hawaii is hard to afford without roommates, so my decision to move back home was made easier by circumstances. I chose to return to Arizona to be what help I could for my mother.

I initially moved into an apartment in the same complex as my mother and carpooled with her to her business. She was struggling with her mother's death and needed help with the day-to-day operations of her nail salon and fashion boutique. I connected with some old friends, but without transportation yet, I spent most of my after-hours partying by the pool with new friends from the complex. No significant boyfriend relationships arose during this time.

My older brother Bob and his wife were having their first child, and things were about to change for the whole family. My mother knew that her business was having problems—would likely close—and agreed that I should go live with my brother and sister-in-law to help with the new baby. I would spend my days being a nanny as "Aunt Shell" and the rest of my time trying to let the new little family have time to themselves.

I decided to make some mental and physical choices that were positive. I went back to college, hired a personal trainer, and started working out. While these decisions were cathartic for me, they intersected with some decisions that would forever change my life, not necessarily for the better.

Chapter 19

Enemy Mine

"Know thy self, know thy enemy. A thousand battles,
a thousand victories."

–Sun Tzu

While I wasn't surrounded by my tribe, the enemy knew where the cracks in the armor were and what would work best on a broken little girl.

Shortly after my salvation, the summer before my junior year in high school my family decided to move to Arizona. The winter we had just experienced in Michigan was brutal, and my mom was done. The road trip to Arizona was a mixed bag for me. Leaving everything I knew where I was beginning to feel safe . . . and leaving everyone I knew behind.

We had fun as a family on the trip and every single thing

we did was a first for us kids. We were in our own little family bubble travelling in our recreational vehicle and staying at campgrounds and truck stops. It was just the five of us. I found the space to breathe a little easier.

We moved to Casa Grande, Arizona, which is half-way between Phoenix and Tucson, where the high school alone had as many students as the entire K-12 of the school system I had just come from.

While my mother remained a devout Catholic her whole life, after her divorce, she did not attend mass as regularly as she once had. She did not choose to attend church with me and my brothers, either.

We arrived in Arizona in July and only had a couple weeks to get ourselves settled, and finding a church home was not on my mom's to do list. We had not been able to attend church for several months before departing Michigan, and I was anxious to find a church home.

I rode my bike several blocks at a time, circling out from our new house in order to see what churches might be nearby. I saw a Baptist church, a Catholic church, and a Pentecostal church and made a mental note to check out the Baptist church, since I had been to the other two as a kid and this one sounded most like my Bible church back in Decatur.

* * *

On my first day of school, while staring at my locker trying to decide where to go, two young ladies walked right up to me and asked me if I knew the Lord as my Savior. There was Jesus. He knew what I needed to grow my relationship with Him in this literal and metaphorical desert.

The love He lavished on me by setting up this divine appointment. I was speechless, and that was a first for me. Tears welled in my eyes as I gave them my story. They, too, acknowledged that our meeting was smack dab in the middle of His will for all three of us.

They commandeered my schedule, locked arms with me, and off we went. They showed me how to find my first class and made me promise to join them for lunch. They were even stationed outside my last class before lunch just to make sure I didn't get lost.

There was a large group of Christians that hung out at lunch every day. They came from every group: jocks, geeks, band, debate, theater. Of course meeting new people always made me cautious, but they were all so friendly, and each one invited me to their church. By a happy coincidence, the two young ladies both happened to attend the Baptist church that I had seen. I considered it serendipity and agreed to meet them the coming Sunday.

The girls and guys would split up after eating and do a Bible study a couple days a week. Having a Bible study with others was new to me. I had delved into the Bible on my own, taking what I learned from the message at church and using my grandparents' encyclopedias for some context. There was always a preacher or a Sunday School teacher who led the way.

This was awesome for me to begin to learn how to read and understand what God had to say to me by reading his word and praying. There was that voice. The one that showed me how to reason and understand when I was two.

It was the beginning of awesome friendships and the discovery of a great church family. I became ensconced in the youth group at Trinity Baptist Church and was on the campus every time the doors were open. And nobody had to drag me.

Trinity Baptist and Decatur Bible both gave me the same church family appeal. We as members of the church were able to participate not only in the service, but directly in a relationship with Jesus. This felt real. This felt like home.

On my way to school a couple times a week, I joined a morning prayer group of high schoolers. I didn't know how to pray or what I was doing, I just loved being with kids my age who loved the Lord. We all prayed conversationally, like we would talk to each other. The fact that we were talking and listening to Jesus was just simple for us. By the time I graduated high school I had become one of the leaders of the group.

Monday night visitation and soul-winning was actually something I looked forward to, in spite of my incredible fear of new people. The adults came with us, but we were going out to visit young people who had come to church or our small group and just see what they were seeking.

The parents were ecstatic that we had come to visit, and they would break out cookies and sodas and give us their living room. Sharing the truth about Jesus was like a salve for my broken little spirit's healing. He had always been there and had given me the healing I was now able to share with others.

Wednesday night youth group was a combination of Bible study and good wholesome fun. For teenagers, in such a small town, it was nice to have an option that didn't involve getting into trouble. Being an athlete, I got invited to the alternate universe regularly. After what I saw as a child in my father, I was good with staying away from drinking and partying.

Along with the morning and evening services on Sundays, I was probably at the church more than the pastor. An older couple in the church took to me, calling me an old soul. They started mentoring me. They were really cool. They were not incredibly strict or legalistic. They understood how the world worked and knew that instilling a robust understanding of the character of God and His word would go farther than lectures about what not to do. It was a fabulous time of growth for me.

* * *

I would meet so many special people who helped my walk with my Lord flourish. I would also meet some who, while my choices are mine to own, totally saw my vulnerability and seized the day.

There were not any purity balls, purity rings, or people discussing purity when I was a teenager. It was understood that sex out of wedlock was a sin, but it was a taboo topic, and parents were supposed to cover that.

The spring semester of my junior year, I met a young guy through a church friend. During that time, we had a lot going on as a family, and it was a time of good and bad stress. I went through a lot of physical and health changes and was not feeling particularly good about myself as a whole.

Jeff was twenty-one and I was sixteen, not that he checked. He knew what to say and how to say it to get what he wanted from a broken, vulnerable virgin. He knew he had to make a declaration of some sort of love without committing. He drew my mom in to his favor. He had been playing this game for several years and was leaving quite a trail of tears. I would later find out that he was specifically seeking the vulnerable virgins who came from broken places. Now, my choices were mine, but he knew what he was doing, and worked it well.

My first sexual experience, other than molestation, was at sixteen years old at the hands of a twenty-one-year-old man. Jeff had a fiancée in Texas who was remaining pure until their marriage. He needed his needs fulfilled and used whoever was at hand. He made sure he had enough time to make us feel he could love us; told us he loved us and worked it from there.

I have never been and wasn't suicidal but wanted to die after it was over. I thought that when I walked into church the next time there would be some sort of mark on my forehead showing what had happened.

He continued to work me for approximately nine months. I found out later that there were many others at the same time. It is divine intervention that I did not contract some kind of sexually transmitted disease.

I did, however, get pregnant. Jeff had frequent flyer miles at Planned Parenthood and knew the routine down pat. It didn't faze him to break out the $200 fee for the abortion, drive me to Phoenix and then back home to fend for myself. Bragging later about how many times he had done this.

It was all a blur. Abortion had only been legal for a short time, and there wasn't the media and information letting me understand that I was ending a human life. They did not talk to me about options. He told them what he wanted, they took his money, and that was that.

* * *

The entire time this was all taking place, I was not sharing any of it with anyone. Especially my friends and youth group. As far as I believed, no one even knew I was having sex. That would have had its own implosion on my currently fragile world.

I came home one day to my mother sitting quietly in the living room with the insert from a birth control packet that I had received after the abortion, unfolded and held up, hiding her face as if looking at a newspaper. Through the ringing in my ears, I felt like I was going to pass out. She asked where I had gotten them and if I wanted to talk about anything. And that was literally my "birds and bees" talk with my mom.

Jeff's treatment of me and the whole situation caused me

to take a stance diametrically opposed to that of my Christian beliefs. I didn't believe I was turning anyone from God, but I was certainly not pointing anyone toward him. I do not confess this to brag. I had been through so much destruction at the hands of men who claimed to love and care for me that I decided that I would control things now.

Chapter 20

Control Freak

"Marvel at what happens when you stop interfering."

–Unknown

Satan saw me coming a mile away. I jumped in the deep end without a single swimming lesson. High school graduation went off without a hitch. Two full-ride scholarships for sports and academics and I was off to college life. I decided to live in the dorms instead of at home. Not that living at home had me making any better choices. This just opened up a world where I was going to be in charge.

My first year of college, I happened to get roommates who were believers. We would do Bible study together and pray together in the morning before class. Our dedication to our schoolwork as well as at least one job kept us with a pretty tight schedule.

This did not, however, preclude us from participating in the school dances and the weekend partying. It was an interesting dynamic, and after what I had been through was not altogether awful. I mean, waking up after drinking is no picnic, but somehow, the way we all created our own little community and we kept each other from total stupidity, it had a bizarre balance to it.

* * *

This was the beginning of an approximately ten-year prodigal stint of doing things my way. My self-inflicted guilt, shame, and embarrassment from the choices I had made that got me here launched me into a period of a broken relationship with my King. I did not denounce Him or deny Him. I simply was not bringing Him glory. I did not blame Him for the things that had happened. I simply decided to make my own ill-advised decisions of how I would let people love me . . . or not.

Once again, I was not listening to His voice. My life was having a five-alarm fire set off, and I was caring for it with a water pistol. I believed that these things were happening because I was allowing people to "love" me, so they could reject me in the first place. How I did not exhaust the grace He lavished upon me in the waiting for me to return to Him was beyond my comprehension.

This period included my first move to California. I imagined I was accomplishing many things . . . in my head. I was moving away from everyone I knew, which gave me a semblance of peace from what I thought others were thinking about me. I thought that taking control of who I engaged with and what happened to me would give me peace. I could not have been more wrong. To this day, I pay for that miscalculation.

I control nothing. My heart paid the price for my arrogance. There was no activity in my relationship with Christ during my time in California. I would come home for holidays and take my mom to midnight Mass at a local Catholic church, and that would be the extent of it.

Moving on from any relationship before any significant connection was keeping me from rejection. It was also keeping me from any meaningful connection or relationships. Not listening to the Holy Spirit counsel I had at my disposal took me on a doctorate-level journey of what not to choose.

* * *

After a couple years in California and two vacations to Hawaii, I decided to shake things up with another move. I secured a job and living arrangements, but finding a church home was still not on the agenda.

While living in Hawaii, I met some special people who are in my life to this day. I again was not active in my relationship with Christ. The decision to live a sexually immoral lifestyle and casually give pieces of myself to people I let have no consequence in my life was tearing at my soul.

I still did not go looking for a church family or seek to get back into and grow my relationship with Jesus. I did, however, start to feel the brokenness of not having anyone who meant something to me in my life. We were created for relationships with our Creator and with others. I was missing the boat on both counts.

While nothing about how I was living would have indicated that I was a twice-born child of God, I did keep being drawn to experiences that showed me He was still chasing after me. My roommates were not overly religious either, but we came together one Christmas and decided we wanted to go to Christmas Eve service.

We found a Bible church near Waikiki Beach that had a candlelight service and was authentically Hawaiian. We prepared Christmas dinner at our place and had one of the more in-depth conversations on our faith that I have had in my lifetime. There was Jesus.

While I did not abandon my current shenanigans, I did recognize and take note of my King running after me. He had never left. He never would. Nothing can separate us from His love. I do not believe that we can lose our salvation either. I just was not walking in his will or fulfilling my purpose.

* * *

I was living in Hawaii on the day I was called and told that my grandmother died. It was the same day the Challenger space shuttle blew up, and this would make the anniversary an announcement in the news for years to come. Mom needed my help and asked me if I would please come home from Hawaii. Other circumstances had my roommates moving out as well, and so I began the transition. I moved back to Arizona about four months later.

My mother had a new boyfriend by the time I moved back. He and a couple of his friends were there for my mom when my grandmother died. He introduced her to marijuana, and there were some other concerning, isolating behaviors that meant I had no space to attempt to be of comfort to my mom.

I became my brother's nanny for his first-born child, which made me feel more connected to family. I did not begin to seek a church family or press into my relationship with Jesus, but I did feel a draw to better relationships. And a little conviction that my current lifestyle was not benefitting any area of my health.

Chapter 21

Solitary Confinement

"We are all sentenced to solitary confinement inside
our own skins, for life."

–Tennessee Williams

In a strange place, at a strange time, with what felt like total
strangers. No one to talk to or advise about the options that
were before me. Everyone in the house was living their own
lives in parallel spaces.

We arrived in Arizona just a couple of weeks before school
would be starting. In Arizona, school started in late August. In
Michigan, we had until the Tuesday after Labor Day. My mom
had found a job at the local hospital as the administrator and
would be on the clock and in a hurry to take us to get situated
for the fall semester of my junior year.

My mother took us kids to the high school to register all of us, and then we were sent to the gym to decide what our schedule was going to look like. There were lines for everything. Various sports teams, school ID, lunch accounts, and each of the areas of study.

Michigan public schools were exceptional at the time, but because of the small size of our school, there was not a plethora of honors or extracurricular classes. They covered the basics well, and the rest of our time was spent competing in some fashion.

We were not informed that Arizona might have different requirements than Michigan and that we might have too much or too little education. I was enrolled in the standard junior classes and Advanced Placement classes where they were available. I was handed a schedule and told to be back on Monday.

While the enormity of the school campus terrified me, typically school was a safe space for me. Being a planner, I took my schedule with the building and classroom numbers on it and made my way around the campus to devise a plan. The teachers in each of the classrooms were astonished to see someone so enthusiastic and were delighted to chat with me about where I had come from and what their expectations were for the students.

* * *

Thanks to the Christian young ladies I met the first day, I was able to meet and become friends with many fellow Christians throughout my classes. New friends made me feel happy for some familiar faces as the school year began.

My Advanced Placement classes had no familiar faces and in fact felt like a hazing ritual at the beginning of every class for a while. The football player who was happy to get acquainted with another outsider made for some comedy relief when I was on awkward overload.

Just as in Michigan, the students who found themselves at the top of the heap had gotten there by their hard work and did not wish to have the applecart tipped. Even the teacher of the AP English class appeared to have already made up her mind who would remain at the top of the current crop of students. It took me the entire first semester to win her over.

Just before the spring semester of my junior year, I had met the young man who would become my first boyfriend. Jeff was twenty-one and was taking classes at the local community college. He explained to me that due to my grades, I could take college classes while still in high school. Because of the number of credits I had brought from Michigan, I also only had a half-day schedule at school for my remaining two years. So, bearing in mind my sports schedule, I enrolled in evening classes.

At this point my mother had bought a laundromat and enlisted us kids as employees. We not only had to sit in the laundromat and clean and help customers, but my mother also got the great idea to offer a laundry service. Some people would just drop off their laundry and pick it up at an appointed time. Others took advantage of delivery service for an extra fee.

I managed to maintain a good grade point average while attending both high school and college and working a rigorous job. This brought me joy to see that I was in fact managing on my own, without my father. However, as my involvement with my new boyfriend deepened and a job was added into the mix, my grades slipped a tad for a couple of the more weighted classes, which caused me to drop to ninth place out of 489 students. I realize this would be considered outstanding by anyone else, but I, on the other hand, considered it the beginning of failure.

My senior year began without the boyfriend and with a new job at McDonald's on the schedule. I continued taking college classes and could now drive myself, since we had a family car that us kids shared. After what I had gone through with the boyfriend, I found myself viewing my academics with a healthier lens.

I still believed in doing my best and setting the bar high; however, I realized that becoming despondent if I received an A- was unhealthy. My senior year was great all-around in that my sports teams did well, and my grades kept me in the top ten of my class, which in Arizona added some more scholarship interest.

Three scholarships were awarded to me at graduation. One for my academic placement and two for sports. All of which were full-ride to the local community college. Since my family lived paycheck-to-paycheck, we did not have the money for any of us to go to college, and therefore scholarships were well-received.

* * *

Since I had been attending community college in the evenings, I felt no trepidation in heading into a new environment. My degree was to be an associate's in business administration. I acquired a job working in the business department on campus, which gave me access to typewriters and word processors for homework and for a paper-writing business I had on the side.

This particular campus had some married housing that was like apartments, and if there were no married students utilizing them, the college offered them to either student body officers or academically gifted students. The apartments were awesome in that they had full bathrooms within the rooms, as well as full-size refrigerators. The buildings of this housing were set apart from the regular dorms, and this situation was great for keeping my roommates and me from even more mischief.

I supported the school sports teams by being the president of the pep club and by dating and encouraging athletes. Thankfully I was involved in a sport for both semesters, which kept my attention on school for the most part.

* * *

My first taste of alcohol, outside of my grandmother's Baptist cough medicine, was in college. I do not recall thinking one way or the other about why I had not drunk up to this point. Nor did I consider the consequences for starting. I was ashamed of myself for having premarital sex and had decided to set aside any need to confirm if my behavior was acceptable, since I was already damaged goods.

Social drinking in college, for me, was confined to the dances and school events that primarily took place on the weekends. This gave me recovery time. and kept alcohol from interfering with my classwork. I also had a workout routine that kept me sweating out the toxins and clearing my brain, which helped me balance my time.

I took full advantage of my two-year scholarships and managed to keep a good grade point average in spite of the introduction of partying. I did not, however, complete my associates degree. However, I passed the entrance exam to the school of hard knocks with flying colors.

Chapter 22

Head Games

"Never play mind games in relationships; the only thing you'll win is loneliness."

–Unknown

Starting my first job at age nine, I had accumulated a lot of skills sets through multiple jobs from childhood through community college. I also competed in college for "Miss Future Business Executive," in which I won locally and regionally and went on to nationals. This competition gave a tremendous amount of development in résumé building and the interview process. I decided to take this wonderful "employee-in-the-making" on the road.

My mother had moved to Tempe to take a better-paying job and continue her college education as well. I moved into an apartment in her complex and set out to find a job. I had utilized a headhunter to find a summer job previously and went back to them to check opportunities. This was when job ads were in print, in a newspaper.

Office Manager for a modular building contractor would be my first full-time job. It would be life-changing both for what I learned and the relationships I built. The construction industry was not for the faint of heart back then, since the typical jargon was like the Wild West. If you were easily offended, you'd better get on the next train back home.

My coworkers and their mates and friends were much better at the ins and outs of all-you-can-eat buffet happy hours than I was. Although this was a skill set I picked up all too readily. I did, however, manage to again keep the damage of the extracurricular activities to the weekend, so that I was efficient at my job and excelled at acquiring raises regularly.

It felt incredible that what I had actually learned in college was readily utilized and applied to my current position. As a lifelong learner, I ate up every other opportunity that came my way to add something to my toolkit. The construction industry was great for a lot of life lessons for future jobs in supporting industries, as well as understanding the ins and outs of home ownership and maintenance.

* * *

A desire to learn new things and see more of the world drove me to look into moving to California. I had met some friends during my college competitions who lived there and needed a roommate. I looked into the job market, reached out to a Los Angeles headhunter, and the ball got rolling quickly.

I took a trip specifically to engage in several interviews and check out where my new living space would be. All three of the companies I interviewed with wanted to hire me. My agent told me to come back and confer with her first so we could shape the best offer. I took a job with an accounting firm that would pay me double what I was currently making in Phoenix.

Two weeks' notice. My mother was heartbroken and pressed me for how soon I would be home to visit. My Arizona friends threw me quite the going-away party, and I was on the road. Once again, I was leaving what I knew for a whole new world. It felt freeing this time. Like, perhaps, I was leaving what I didn't want everyone else to know about me behind.

Working for a Big 8 accounting firm in downtown Los Angeles required me to put my big girl pants on quickly. I soaked up information like a sponge and have utilized the tricks of the trade my entire working career. Accounting has been the underpinning of my skill sets and has helped me clinch jobs that might have otherwise seemed unattainable.

It was still business as usual. No deep, meaningful relationships were going to have the opportunity to manipulate or reject me. I am confident that I cast aside some wonderful men who may have even included the man God had in mind for me, in the name of protecting myself.

I made incredible money for my age and decided to try visiting some places. After a trip to Hawaii with some friends and my mom, I was in love. Six months later, I went again with the same friends and had a hidden agenda. I checked the papers for the job market and devised a plan.

* * *

I flew to Hawaii with a one-way ticket and a cheap hotel reservation. I reached out to a headhunter the first day and got a job in, you guessed it, accounting for American Express military banking. They handle the banking on all of the US military bases in Asia and the South Pacific.

This became a learning experience more on other cultures and opened my brain to a whole new world. It had culinary advantages as well. The cost of living in Hawaii was off the charts, and I decided an additional part-time job doing something fun was necessary. I went to talk to the couple who had a travel agency and had helped me when I visited on vacation.

I began part-time with them selling tours, etc . . . As I worked for them, I realized that they were doing all their business in stacks of paper. Well, Lotus 1-2-3, a new computer spreadsheet, had come out, and it was all the rage. So, we struck a deal to bring them into the 20th century and keep me from living paycheck-to-paycheck. As their Quality Control Manager, we began to grow exponentially.

My boss would hand me a stack of business cards and send me to the world-famous happy hour across the street at a bar called Moose McGillicuddy's. The next day, there would be a line out our front doors. Every luau, tour, hotel, airline—you name it—would reach out to my boss and have him send me to their place to evaluate and bring on board their opportunity. I was sent to every island, every event, free-of-charge. Needless to say, this was hands-down my favorite job of a lifetime, outside of being a mom.

My roommates began leaving or getting married, and Hawaii is not affordable without having partners-in-crime. I was staring the possibility of having to move back to Arizona in the face when fate lent a hand. On January 28th, 1986, the Challenger space shuttle blew up. It was also the day my grandmother passed away. My mother was devastated and requested I come home to Arizona.

I am a dutiful daughter and was definitely going to move

back. However, I did drag my feet. I loved my job, and since my boss was closing in on retirement years, I thought I had a future in Hawaii. By June, I had sold every possession that couldn't fit in my luggage and moved back home to Arizona. A part of me felt like this was a step backward.

* * *

Back in Mesa, Arizona, I moved into the same apartment complex as my mother, again. She needed emotional support and someone to take some shifts at her business, The Eye for Beauty. My mother always had an entrepreneurial spirit. Her accounting business out of our home as kids. The laundromat when I was in high school. And now a retail nail salon and fashion boutique. All this while she was still working an accounting job at a large catalog retailer.

She taught me so much. I wish she were still alive for me to tell her more about this revelation as I am walking through this part of my journey again. The business was struggling at the time I came to help. In fact, it only survived about five more months. At this point, my older brother was due to have his first child. My sister-in-law did not wish to give up working, so they presented a plan for me to become the nanny, receive a vehicle, and be able to go to college to finish up in the evenings.

As a nanny, I was definitely more like Fran Dresher than Mary Poppins. However, my little niece had me wrapped around her finger from the word go. We developed a great rhythm where my brother and sister-in-law headed off to work, and the day belonged to me and my niece. They would come home to a clean house, a dinner made, and a very happy baby, and I would head out to school.

After approximately a year, and with their second baby on the way, they decided my services would no longer be required.

So, through my dear friend from the modular business, I found a job as a leasing coordinator for a copier company.

This time my after-work activities turned to the gym and time with my trainer. It would be here that my greatest testing would come to bear.

Chapter 23

It's My Body and I'll Cry if I Want To

"You are not your own; you were bought at a price.
Therefore, honor God with your bodies."

(1 Cor 6:20)

We left Michigan with my heart and my body weighing exponentially more than I would have liked. During my childhood and teen years, I was a stress-eater. My heart was hurting, and the stress of leaving everything and everyone I knew made for a lethal combination for my physique. My heart had not learned how to comfort itself, and eating was the dopamine hit it required.

We had bought a recreational vehicle for our trek to

Arizona and took our time, stopping to see various friends of my parents. A situation that I have never shared with anyone took place at the home of a dear friend of my mother. I was approached by a grown man of forty years. I was fifteen years old and did not have the emotional stability to deal with this. Fortunately, divine intervention kept him from succeeding in molesting me, and I was able to get out of it without physical harm. Emotionally was another matter. We headed into Arizona with my vulnerability exposed and any ability I had at discernment in tatters.

The first order of business when we arrived was getting enrolled in school. Particularly engaged with sports tryouts. After signing up for everything, a sports physical was next on the agenda. I was familiar with the routine. Height, weight, blood pressure. Basic once-over of our ability to stand without falling over. Every orifice looked into for no apparent reason.

Being my first sports physical in Arizona, there was a new set of physician's notes that were startling. He looked up my nose and remarked, "You aren't from here, are you?" Startling, because why would looking up my nose tell him that? He indicated that people who had been in Arizona very long had developed "valley fever" conditions in their noses and sinus cavities, and apparently I looked healthy.

So, cleared for duty, I was off to volleyball tryouts with a team and coaches I had never met. I had never had a true athlete's body, but I did have the heart of a champion. We had gone to the state championships in both volleyball and softball in Michigan, and I believed in myself enough to have confidence that I would at least turn in a good showing. Even if this had not been the case, this was one area I knew I had the skill sets and would definitely give it my all.

Because of the open nature of gymnasiums, ones in Arizona

were serviced by swamp coolers instead of air conditioning, at least in the '80s. Being a sturdy young woman with the metabolism of a Crock-Pot, I was sweltering. At one point during the tryouts, I was concentrating more on coming out of them alive than making the team. But make the team I did, and I began to feel like my surroundings were familiar and a safer space, for the moment.

* * *

I was still carrying more weight than I would have liked and was self-conscious. Buying school clothes for that year was another fun adventure. Casa Grande was a small town, but along the main drag there was a Kmart and a Sears where school clothes shopping could be done. So, praise the Lord, no homemade "outfits." Levi's 501s had been introduced to the fashion world, and I settled into a kind of female "Fonz" look in T-shirts with 501 jeans and Converse sneakers, topped off with a ponytail.

In the second semester of my junior year, I met my soon-to-be boyfriend. Jeff was skilled at looking for the type of vulnerability and naivete that was my natural state. He knew what he needed to say to get what he wanted. He made me feel wanted and loved and even incorporated my mother in the whole charade. We did actually go on dates, and he played the part of a good Christian boy . . . until he didn't.

His ultimate goal to have sex with as many young virgins as he could was always forefront in his mind and the guideline of all activities and conversations. He got me to his house indicating that we were once again having dinner with his parents, but they were conveniently absent.

The move to his bedroom was well rehearsed and came with assurances that it was just to listen to music. We had kissed before, so that was something that he could lead with and was comfortable. Starting to undress both himself and me was new.

Taking no for an answer was unacceptable, and he pressed through my protests, telling me that he loved me and that this would be how I could prove I loved him in return. If I did not acquiesce, I clearly did not feel the same and shame was being imposed. If I rejected him, wasn't I the same as everyone who had ever promised they loved me but didn't?

I could not hear the voice of Jesus over the sound of my own screaming inside my head. Every fiber of my being knew that this was not good. My mind knew better. My body was freaking out and shutting down at the same time. My heart desperately wanted someone who was saying "I love you" to mean it. Any resolve I had left dissipated.

At this time my youth group did not have purity vows or even conversations about sex. For me it was the awful flash-backs of a twenty-three-year-old man molesting five-year-old me against my will. This man was twenty-one and I was sixteen. He did not take no for an answer.

Jeff only took off his shorts and my jeans. As with my child-hood molestation, he only needed access. He forced my legs apart against my protests and assured me that he loved me and this would be good for us.

Losing my virginity was painful and lasted all of two minutes. He seemed elated and ambivalent to my feelings. He got up and put on his shorts. He tossed me my jeans and told me to get dressed and leave, since his parents would be home soon. There were no more "I love you's" or kisses before my departure. I was ushered to the door.

This wound felt the same as when I was five. My abuser then did not say, "I love you," but that did not make what my boyfriend did any less traumatic. The devastation was mine alone to bear. I did not tell a soul. This wound would require stitches that I did not soon receive.

* * *

Oddly, he had in mind to get more sex from me, at least for a little while. The rejection I had felt all my life caused me to accept even his pathetic attention as better than no attention at all. In a matter of a couple weeks, I began to feel horrifically sick. I was exhausted all the time and did not feel like getting up each morning. Feeling like I was going to throw up all day long had me concerned as to what I might have caught.

He knew immediately what was happening. He had been there before. I had not had consensual sex before him. I had no earthly clue about birth control or what it even was. Not that he asked. It appeared that I got pregnant from my first experience.

He was a familiar face at Planned Parenthood and knew exactly what to do. Back then Roe v. Wade had just been passed, and there was no one protesting or making sure we got ultrasounds or any information besides how an abortion was simple and easy. I was being carried along and did not fully realize what was happening until it was over.

After paying them and being checked in, I was put in a room full of women who were not saying a word. No one was making eye contact. Several were crying. Women who I believe were nurses came and went, giving us pills that they said would help with pain. A nurse called my name and led me to a room with a table, like a doctor's office.

I was told to undress from the waist down. Ironic that being unclad from the waist down is what got me there in the first place. They had me get on the table, put my feet in stirrups, and cover myself with a paper towel blanket. As I understand it, now they put women to sleep for an abortion. This is not how I experienced it. I was left wide awake and only slightly drowsy from the pain medication.

I had never had an annual women's exam and certainly never anything involving equipment that "opens" things up. I could not see exactly what the doctor was using due to my paper towel blanket. Every bit of the procedure was painful. From the gigantic needle they used to stab something inside to help with pain to whatever they used to pry me open further. No one in the room would look at me or attempt to comfort me.

Now the tearing at my body and soul would begin. The doctor kept shoving something in and out that sounded like a vacuum cleaner. I felt like I would pass out from the pain, and it felt like it went on for a lifetime. Two nurses put what looked like a huge maxi pad between my legs and assisted me in putting my underpants back on. They sat me up and ushered me into a room that looked like the first one I was in, only now everyone was crying.

Truthfully, I did not fully realize that what I had just participated in was the ending of a life. I thought that having to hide that I was having sex was enough of a nightmare. It would be years before I understood fully what I had done or even tell another person. I did, however, feel every bit of the fact that I had been awake for something being sucked out of my body. My soul and my body understood what I had just sacrificed. This wound remained open for twenty-six years.

* * *

The summer before my senior year in high school was very stressful, both good and bad, and tumultuous. I was feeling excruciating pain every time I ate, and I lost fifty pounds in four weeks. It was painful and really scary, but awesome. I looked good and managed to maintain my energy. It was, however, not a fun way to lose weight and keep it off.

My mother was beside herself and was working with experts at the University of Arizona to find out what was happening. I, on the other hand, was not hoping for a cure. I was taken to the University of Arizona Medical Center in Tucson, and the medical team informed me that they were going to give me a barium enema—oh, joy! —and depending on what they found, possibly send a camera on a length of hose down my throat. To my chagrin, the hose was necessary.

They made me gargle with Novocain, which, by the way, tastes disgusting, and then informed me that all of this needed to take place while I was awake so they could see what was truly happening in my stomach. They even positioned the monitor so I could see, too!

They discovered an ulcer and the duodenal muscle clamped firmly shut. I was told that normally it would have caused food to back up and I would have gained weight. My body shoved it through in excruciating fashion and caused dramatic weight loss. I asked if they had to fix it and would it really be so bad to let me drop a little more weight. Needless to say, they had a relatively easy fix. Muscle relaxer medication for the stomach muscle. I was told to stop being anxious for the emotional portion of how my body reacted.

In addition to the dramatic weight loss, circumstances arose that brought into question the need for the insanely thick glasses, with bifocals, that I wore. A family that I babysat for in my church had learned that I had not had a proper eye exam in a while, and they anonymously sent my pastor to tell me that I was getting an eye exam and contacts and that I was not to rob the family of the blessing of giving this to me.

 172

So, off I went to my eye exam. I had indeed not been tested correctly and would have had much thinner glasses, but I took to contacts like a fish to water. With each person brought through and to my life, my King was showing me His grace and that I was not alone. He was always there. Drawing my attention in a thousand little ways that He knew would speak to me.

I had had long hair that came down to my hiney most of my life. I decided to get a "Dorothy Hamill" cut that summer, and along with the contact lenses and dramatic weight loss, created a buzz that a new student had come to school.

It turns out that we are so magnificently created that our bodies will adapt processes trying to save us. Anxiousness, of both the good and bad variety, caused my body to go on defense to protect itself.

What I had been through to this point in life had not been totally dealt with, and it was starting to show. I would go on hanging onto all my secrets and letting anxiety have sway over how my head and my heart made choices.

Chapter 24

Body Work

"When you touch a body, you touch the whole person,
the intellect, the spirit, and the emotions."

–Jane Harrington

A whole new world. While I had attended classes at the community college during my junior and senior years in high school, I had not lived on campus. The actual campus of the Coolidge location of Central Arizona College was basically out in the middle of nowhere. In the desert, at the base of a mountain without any sign of civilization for ten miles.

Across the street, in the middle of the desert, literally the only structure in sight, was a convenience store. Conveniently located junk food and alcohol. I had a car, and this made me everyone's "best friend." They all wanted a ride, did not feel the need to compensate me for the fuel, and thought being my friend should be payment enough.

I was industrious and had several part-time and seasonal jobs that filled my coffers without being obvious. My main gig was working in the business department, which gave me access to "word processors" and typewriters. This job kept me on track for my own homework and also provided an avenue for me to type up other students' papers for additional cash.

As an athlete, I was involved in the boosters and student body associations. The ombudsman for the student athletes also came into opportunities for event work and seasonal jobs that fit around their sports schedules.

The local Elks Lodge had special events quarterly, and they needed servers. They specifically asked the college for females in particular. It did not occur to me that this should have felt creepy. The members, in fact, behaved themselves for the most part and just enjoyed the view. They paid twenty bucks an hour, allowed us to partake of the meal that was served when we were done with our shift, and had a full bar in their lodge and told us we could utilize that as well.

Since I was the first event worker they hired and they liked my organizational skills, they had me as the point person to make arrangements for hiring the rest of the servers for each event. I got twenty-five bucks an hour for my efforts and became extremely popular among the female athletes.

Because of my scholarships, none of my newfound cash was necessary for any school expenses and therefore helped me accumulate a healthy stash. I had been driving my older brother's car while he was at Navy boot camp, and he was back now to retrieve it on his way to where he would be stationed in San Diego. The time to buy my first car was at hand.

At eighteen years old, I had found a car in an ad in the newspapers for sale at a dealership in Phoenix. I spoke to someone over the phone and made the decision. My mother lived nearby in Tempe, so I asked her to meet me there for support. It was a stick shift, and I had not driven one in a while, so I asked her to take it around the block with me, and then I hopped in the driver seat and gave it a whirl.

My first car, a 1976 Ford Pinto hatchback, was orange/red in color, and you could see me coming for a mile. It served me well and could hold everything I owned. Which was perfect for the journey that was on the horizon.

***

It was time. My scholarships had been used up and I had no money or desire to stay there any longer. I packed up my things and headed to Tempe and the apartment complex where my mother lived. I rented a studio apartment and made my next move to contact an employment agency.

The first company I interviewed with offered me the job on the spot, and it was a great opportunity for a nineteen-year-old. The job was in the construction industry and that meant early hours and therefore plenty of time for after-work shenanigans. My coworkers were a plethora of information in regard to free happy hour buffets and cheap drinks.

I enjoyed the company of men at this time but was not going to let any of them "love" me. I cannot say that I did not enjoy myself with my new friends. However, there was not much that was healthy for me physically that was going on and it began to show up in my shape and energy levels.

We are so beautifully created that we actually have to work overtime to destroy our health. This is how well we are created with backup systems that will fight for our life. I would imagine at this time I was killing off more brain cells than I was generating. A disparity that would get my attention.

* * *

No truly meaningful male relationships were built at this time. I did, however, make friendships that would come in and out of my life up to this day. One friend from college reached out about getting an apartment in Los Angeles for his new job, and would I be interested in being a roommate?

Striking out on my own had not given me pause in the past but had only been to leave home for college. This would be a different state where I had no community other than a college acquaintance. I was feeling like I was stagnant in that I worked every day, socialized every night and weekend, and wasn't really making anything of myself.

I found an employment agency in Los Angeles through some connections in Phoenix and reached out to see what the job market was like. The agent had three jobs off the top of her head where she wanted to set up interviews. The dates were set, and it gave me an opportunity to see the apartment as well.

We accepted a job with an accounting firm in downtown LA, and my apartment was in Van Nuys. Not a short distance apart; however, there was an express bus that picked up literally in front of my apartment complex.

To my mother's chagrin, the move was on. I once again packed everything I owned into my hatchback and was off on a new adventure. It was exhilarating and terrifying as I crossed the state line into California knowing this was going to be my new home for the foreseeable future.

* * *

The '80s in California were a bit of "Mr. Toad's Wild Ride." I settled into a routine at my new job and that included kicking off the weekends with happy hour in a downtown establishment. Accountants are more fun than they look. There wasn't anyone in the mix that looked interesting as a date, but there were several people who became my regular partners in crime.

I adopted the same philosophy regarding dating and did not let anyone get past all of the walls. Most of my time was spent absorbing as much knowledge as I could about not only accounting but also about each of the industries we were representing as clients.

Friends from college who lived in California would stay with me for the weekend and we would go to concerts, clubs, or even short trips together. I also established friendships with two unlikely characters at my firm: a much older gentleman and a college intern who was only a couple years younger than me.

The younger guy literally looked like Tom Cruise in *Risky Business* and had started a side hustle distributing cocaine to other wealthy college kids. Cocaine was huge in the '80s, and he had no shortage of customers. He introduced the older gentleman and me to his product line and always had a supply whenever we would head out to happy hour or clubs.

Some guys in college had offered me a hit of marijuana, and, not understanding what it was, I took one. Looking like a sort of cigarette, it was equally disgusting, and the resultant "dopiness" was unpleasant, so I never wished to continue using.

Cocaine, on the other hand, was a different kind of high. It was upbeat and offset the drowsy effects of alcohol. It was a bit of an appetite suppressant and came with some weight-loss benefits as well. Week-in and week-out for approximately a year, this was my routine.

At the time, I did not see a downside. Yes, there were mornings when didn't feel so great, but a little hit of cocaine and I was back on my feet. I was having fun with my friends, and no one was making promises they wouldn't keep, so in my warped little brain, I was safe.

* * *

My current employment offered quarterly bonuses that opened up new adventures. My California friends from college suggested a trip to Hawaii, and the planning began. How my mother ended up joining us is not really clear to me. It was an incredible trip and instigated the desire to do it again six months later.

This time I had recon in mind. It was just my friends and me, and I was going to do some investigation into what it was like and what it would take to live in Hawaii. I grabbed a newspaper and saw enough job opportunities and apartment options to settle the decision.

I gave my roommate and my employer two months' notice and began the planning. This time my little hatchback wouldn't do the trick. My mom came to Los Angeles to a going away party my two partners in crime were throwing, and I gave her the car to take home with her.

The next morning, hungover a bit and utilizing the last of the cocaine that my buddy had given me as a going-away present, I headed to the airport with a one way ticket to Hawaii. No plan B. This was going to work and be an adventure of a lifetime.

* * *

A familiar face at the Honolulu airport made everything about this adventure even more fun. My older brother was in the Navy, and his ship had been relocated from San Diego to Pearl Harbor on Oahu a couple months before my trip. He took me and my steamer trunk to my home for the week, a hotel in Waikiki.

On the Monday following my arrival, I accepted a job and got a referral to some ladies who needed another roommate to split the costs of an apartment. My one-way ticket and no backup plan had paid off. My wide-eyed optimism had no idea what was about to hit me.

Listening to my own advice and continuing with the plan to "protect" myself, I headed into the Waikiki nightlife scene with blinders on. Bill came out of nowhere. A Marine with a charming smile who could sell ice cubes to Eskimos. He had me at hello.

Alarm bells were ringing. Red flags were frantically waving. All I heard was, "Do you want to go for a walk on the beach?" Sold. He was ever-so-dreamy. In all honesty, I don't believe he was seeking to destroy my heart. He was doing what every other young man in his twenties was doing. He was having fun with as many people as possible before having to grow up.

That being said, he did have my heart and it was indeed shattered beyond what I thought could be restored. This time it felt like there would be no more love for me. I was stupid enough to think that I could continue to give myself away and not be entangled. Our bodies do not understand that concept. Each time a bond is formed, and a piece of my soul given away.

* * *

Upon finding out that my grandmother had passed away and my mother needed me, I sold or gave away everything that would not fit in my steamer trunk and bought a one-way ticket back to Arizona. With gaping fresh wounds left by my dreamy Marine, I headed back home to help my family. My mom needed me both literally to help in her business and to also help her find her footing after her loss.

Reeling from my own magnitude of grief, I am not sure that helping my mother was successful. Her business was going to close, and she was going to stay with her day job. My brother's first child was born, and he and his wife both wanted to go back to work, so a deal was struck for me to be the nanny.

My body was sending up flares for help. I was at least thirty pounds overweight and had little or no energy to handle the Arizona heat. I stopped drinking for a time when I got to Arizona, and now I needed to do some body work to promote more healing. I found a gym and a trainer through my sister-in-law's brother.

While these were all good things, it would be at this gym that I would once again let my guard down. I would not be listening to my Jesus. I exposed an already open wound to salt. My future was taking a trajectory of my own choosing.

While my body was so wonderfully created that it had been mending and healing all my life, I was making choices with that body that were tearing the scabs off my heart and soul. I was not listening to any sane voices. I was not consulting my Comforter. I was giving away pieces of myself that could never be retrieved.

At this gym, I would meet the man that would become my husband. My Jesus would use everything about this relationship to gather my attention. His sheep know His voice and He calls them by name. The metamorphosis of healing that began at the first blow when I was two years old and continued in the midst of every wound, would now find me in need of intensive care. Care that only my Creator could provide.

Epilogue

My story. His story. Our Story. The wounds lay open. Some scar tissue has formed. But this is not the end. This is the first twenty-five years, transparent and vulnerable. So incredibly raw and difficult to think about, let alone write down. Some of the actors, both good and bad, are still alive and may have something to say. I have spoken the truth. The truth as I lived it.

The intricate infrastructure that was established to help me begin healing the wounds and reconcile it all has been in place all these decades. In some cases, my choices were what I understood and knew how to handle, even if they continued my journey down the path that had caused total devastation in the first place.

My King has never left me. He did, however, keep His promise that I had been granted free will just like everyone else. What I did with that free will was mine to own. He was always there to pick me up. To make sure I understood the why. His grace and love for me are all that held me together, sometimes barely by a thread.

I have been the victim of abuse. I am not a victim. I have made choices that furthered that abuse at the hands of others. Again, not a victim. My story is being told so that the world, myself, and others who have walked my path can understand what we put together; emotionally, spiritually, mentally and physically to live. To understand exactly what happens in our little minds and hearts to propel us forward, as opposed to feeling the need for it all to end.

The world offers me the choices of being a victim and spiraling into depression and self-pity or abandoning who I was created to be and adopting its version of what someone like me should choose after what I have been through. I don't hate all men or believe that all of them are abusers. I don't want to be comforted and guided into a same-sex lifestyle because a few evil men betrayed me.

Well-meaning Christians offer the position that everything that happened to me because of my own sin and the sin of my forefathers. They posit that these are the just consequences I deserve, and that I need to confess and forgive and move on.

My King, Savior, and Creator was not consulted for any of the preceding "advice" and thankfully has been my real Counselor and Comforter since before I was knit together in my mother's womb. The world and Christians are fully human. What they have to offer needs to be viewed through that lens. Ultimately, my faith worldview is what kept me from taking my life as a victim or in shame. It also kept my own evil choices from totally ending my relationship with my King.

I do not tell my story to brag or to justify any of my behaviors. I tell it because my King asked me to. Actually told me to. In Romans 8:28, He promises that "all things work together for good, for those whom he loves and called according to His purpose."

I truly believe that if anyone who has walked my path could have even a little light shed on what it all generated within us to survive, that would be worth the telling. Those in the world around us, who we are in relationships with, could benefit from understanding why we do what we do as well.

Butterfly Stitches is about what happened to me. It is not who I am. Who I am is the culmination of what my Creator and I constructed in my heart and mind to reconcile twenty-five years of choices and consequences. I got saved at age fourteen, but I truly believe that my King was with me all the way, giving me a mind and heart that was set on him to understand what was happening. Truly hearing from Him at the age of two began the lifelong healing of the wounds to my heart, soul, mind, and body.

The healing, the recovery, the "working together for good" has been a magnificent journey. Now you know the beginning of our story. Next you will know the fulfillment of my healing journey. Then you can hear your healing, Outloud.

Acknowledgments

My life is not possible without my Lord and Savior Jesus Christ. We have dispensed with subtlety and share a level of transparency that is freeing. He is my counselor, my healer, and my redeemer. This is Our story.

Through the telling of our story, my Jesus showed me that in order for me to accept His redemption, I had to believe it was available for everyone. He told me that my father's redemption would come as a result of this telling. I have to acknowledge that the redemption of my abusers is possible, especially in light of what I have received.

I struggle for the words to tell the world what my momma meant to me. She has gone to be with the Lord and will not get to see my story told. So much of my story, both in the living and surviving, would not have been possible without her. None of us deserved what has been told here. After she extracted us from the horrors, she never once spoke about it or badly about our father. My momma was the strongest woman I have ever known, and I miss her every day.

My brothers, Robert and John, were eyewitnesses. There was no other choice to write my Foreword. There is no other choice when I need someone who understands how I am, who I am, and how I am still standing. I reserve the right to tease the dickens out of each of you and receive the same with open arms.

My beautiful baby girl Maya has been and always will be my inspiration. She is my Peanut, and oh how my heart burst upon her arrival. She is the love of my life and the ultimate reason I deeply, truly understand God's unconditional love for us.

Bob Goff and Kimberly Stuart—I can barely say your names without crying. I had no idea what a book coach does and literally no expectations when we met with the exception of believing you would tell me to set my manuscript on fire and start over. Your senses of humor are so tightly aligned with mine that it is both frightening and thrilling to find a kindred spirit. Bob, every time you said, "you need to . . .," I left our conversation needing a defibrillator. You showed me how to take my story to those the Lord knew would need it. Thank you from the bottom of my heart. Kimberly, the tender love and care with which you held my fragile heart leaves me without words. You made me feel safe. You made me feel loved, and in my universe among the humans, that has been in short supply. Thank you for letting me be who I was created to be and laughing in all the right places. I love you, sweet sister.

My sweet copyeditor Alice did not know what she was getting into when Hurricane Michele showed up thinking her manuscript only required some "tweaking." She was patient and polite and always led with the positives. Clearly, we made it through, and she has been an invaluable addition to the "Michele the author" team.

Lindsay, my galactically talented photographer, had my vision from the jump. Another beautiful human that the Lord gave me, who has walked a fair portion of my journey. We were a balm for each other's soul, and I can't wait to shoot our next book cover. My niece Amber, who has a makeup kit with several shades of "blood," prepared me for my cover photoshoot. Another soul who knew immediately what we were going to do. I love you ladies and how you helped me keep my voice.

A precious young lady who went to school with my Peanut,

Lauren, worked her artist magic on my photos to attempt a process never seen before. She did her research, and when she brought the price tag to me, we both almost fainted. She had a magnificent suggestion of perhaps using this technique for a limited edition run of *Butterfly Stitches* once the book is out and a fabulous hit. I loved her thinking, and it is not out of the question. I love my smoke butterfly wings that you made a reality.

My marvelous designer, also a Michelle, worked her magic with my cover design. She took the simple vision that my King gave to me and made it shine. Her font and color choices were spot on and no second options were necessary. I gave her dealers choice on some interior symbols and layout and was thrilled with the results. She went above and beyond on both her work and her support and encouragement. I am ecstatic to have her on the team and already have her on board for the Part 2.

The writer's groups I belong to online have brought me so many friendships and with people I have never met in person. The support and cheering section we are for one another is incredible. There is plenty of room for all our stories out there and we all can't make it alone. Thank you all for your generous support.

Friends and family who have shown interest and the desire to hear my story are too many to number. Thank you all for your words of encouragement. Especially my "focus group" ladies, and you know who you are. You all have seen the "after" picture to this life I have lived and gotten a front row seat to my King Jesus' healing. Thank you for sticking around for the encore.

About the Author

Michele is an expert bean-counter by day. In addition to her work as a bookkeeper, her superpowers and side hustles include pastry chef and author-in-training. She has been told she has "sass," which she deploys regularly. She has with exponential joy finished her first book, *Butterfly Stitches*, and is working on the sequel. According to her King, she apparently has several other books in her. At 61, she has launched a podcast and is having the time of her life.

She is an enthusiastic traveler, foodie, smart alec, and lover of her King, Jesus. Michele lives in Mesa, Arizona, with her daughter, who is lovingly known as Peanut.

Michele would love to engage with you through any and all media. She is also available for speaking engagements and retreats.

www.michelevrabel.com
IG: @sweetartbyshelly

Don't miss out on the sequel to *Butterfly Stitches*!